COME
AND DIE

FOREWORD BY GARY WILKERSON

COME AND DIE

DYING TO SELF AND LIVING FOR CHRIST

JOSHUA WEST

AMBASSADOR INTERNATIONAL
GREENVILLE, SOUTH CAROLINA & BELFAST, NORTHERN IRELAND

www.ambassador-international.com

COME AND DIE

Dying to Self and Living for Christ
©2021 by Joshua West
All rights reserved

ISBN: 978-1-64960-123-0
eISBN: 978-1-64960-173-5
Cover Design by Hannah Linder Designs
Interior Typesetting by Dentelle Design

Unless otherwise indicated, all Scripture quotations taken from The ESV® Bible (The Holy Bible, English Standard Version®). ESV® Text Edition: 2016. Copyright © 2001 by Crossway, a publishing ministry of Good News Publishers. The ESV® text has been reproduced in cooperation with and by permission of Good News Publishers. Unauthorized reproduction of this publication is prohibited. All rights reserved.

Scripture marked KJV taken from The King James Version, The Authorized Version. Public Domain.

Scripture marked NIV taken from THE HOLY BIBLE, NEW INTERNATIONAL VERSION®, NIV® Copyright © 1973, 1978, 1984, 2011 by Biblica, Inc.® Used by permission. All rights reserved worldwide.

Scripture marked NASB taken from the NEW AMERICAN STANDARD BIBLE®, Copyright © 1960,1962,1963,1968,1971,1972,1973,1975,1977,1995 by The Lockman Foundation. Used by permission.

AMBASSADOR INTERNATIONAL
Emerald House
411 University Ridge, Suite B14
Greenville, SC 29601, USA
www.ambassador-international.com

AMBASSADOR BOOKS
The Mount
2 Woodstock Link
Belfast, BT6 8DD, Northern Ireland, UK
www.ambassadormedia.co.uk

The colophon is a trademark of Ambassador, a Christian publishing company.

DEDICATED TO:

The King of glory Jesus Christ: may Your name be known and praised in all the Earth and may every drop of my life be poured out like a drink offering for Your glory.

To every God-fearing pastor who stands behind a pulpit week after week and preaches the sacred words of Scripture without worldly gimmicks or the fear of man and proclaims the whole counsel of God.

To Jennifer McKinney: you are a true missionary who has given your entire life to take the Gospel to the people of Asia; there is no one in this life I admire more than you. You are an inspiration to me. Your life shines beautifully for the glory of God.

To my mother Rachelle: you are my rock. You have always been and will always be my hero.

To my beautiful wife, Kiara: you are my songbird, my sermon sounding board, and my best friend. Walking beside you is the greatest privilege of my life. Always you and only you.

TABLE OF CONTENTS

FOREWORD 9

INTRODUCTION 15

CHAPTER 1
DON'T SKIP THE GOSPEL 19

CHAPTER 2
THE PURSUIT OF HAPPINESS 31

CHAPTER 3
CONFORMING TO HIS IMAGE 41

CHAPTER 4
COME AND DIE 61

CHAPTER 5
WALKING BY THE SPIRIT 77

CHAPTER 6
WORSHIP AND FELLOWSHIP 91

CHAPTER 7

THE EVIDENCE OF A GOSPEL-TRANSFORMED LIFE 101

CHAPTER 8

HOLINESS 125

CHAPTER 9

THE SUFFICIENCY OF SCRIPTURE 147

CHAPTER 10

TO LIVE IS CHRIST; TO DIE IS GAIN 167

CHAPTER 11

THE DAY OF THE LORD 179

CHAPTER 12

THE REWARD OF HIS SUFFERINGS 191

FOREWORD

When we set a hand to our keyboard as a writer, we can take one of two directions. The first and most tempting is to impress our readers, thinking of what might make for a good-selling book. This is not the direction a man of God will take. It might be the route of the so-called preacher who is more of a TED Talk presenter, or a hyped-up, self-help, positive-thinking, so-called pastor; or it might be the approach of the "peddler" of the Word of God, who is afraid to offend, wants to please everyone, and ends up writing such a soft, fluffy, non-confronting word that many readers may be impressed but none are convicted, corrected, challenged or changed.

The second approach to put word to page requires abandoning oneself to the higher calling of the Gospel of Jesus Christ. This direction is demanding. It first requires we have been deeply immersed in the presence of God. It is in this place that the Spirit reveals the deep things of God (1 Cor. 2:10). It is quite easy to write to impress, but it is impossible to write the deep things of God without being with God, studying God, seeking God, knowing God, and hearing from God by His Spirit and through His Word. It is in this second approach that we find a high view of God, rather than the common, low view. It is here we find the majesty, transcendence, and glory of God in magnificent splendor.

Choosing the title *Come and Die: Dying to Self and Living for Christ* is a dead giveaway of which route Joshua West has taken. It is a dangerous title, as many readers may take a pass, recoiling at the thought of dying to self. I hope they don't, for if they pick up this book and read, it would not be long before they realized that this seemingly negative title actually yields the most positive of messages and the only path to abundant life. If they read this book, they will hear things not often said in the modern pulpit, and readers' ears may need to readjust, the way our eyes do when we've been in the dark for so long and a light is turned on. We exist in the dark of a Christian culture that has borrowed a therapy narrative that has permeated everything around us. Rather than confronting the self-help, self-absorbed, self-seeking culture, the Church has become its chaplain. The message in many pulpits is a worldly one, sugarcoated with a few Scriptures and a closing prayer. We need writers who turn on the light in this darkened culture and our dim churches. Joshua has done just that in this book.

Come and Die takes us on a biblically based, Spirit-led, Gospel-driven, Jesus-centered journey of discipleship. It is important because it is different. It bucks the trend of moralistic legalism, as well as therapeutic pop psychology so prevalent today among evangelicals. Self-effort, cloaked in the guise of a therapeutic or moralistic approach to Christian living, will leave a believer defeated, frustrated, and wondering if Christianity really works. You might wonder if I am touting a book that is negative, dreary, preachy, or condemning. Quite the opposite is true. This book is full of abundant life, unquenchable joy, and inexhaustible hope. It is filled with immovable promises of God that lead to fruitful living and overwhelming blessings. Joshua writes of gaining our true life by abandoning old ways of living.

Yet attaining these blessings is not presented as our primary purpose in life or even our primary purpose for coming to God. These joys are but the fallout of a life given over fully to God, the fruits of discipleship and abandoning the totality of our lives to Jesus. As a book and, more importantly, as a lifestyle, *Come and Die* is not a works-based program. What you are about to read calls for a death—not of joy, life, peace, or freedom, but rather of sin, of a Satan-controlled life, of love for a world that gives no peace, and, ultimately, of death itself.

Keep reading Gospel-drenched books like Joshua's, and you will soon be living a Gospel-drenched life. Seek writings that keep your focus on Jesus and leave you focused on Jesus, teachings that view the Gospel through the correct end of the telescope, magnifying Christ rather than leaving us with a minimized view of His glory. Study how to achieve your destiny, and you are likely to place Christ on the periphery as you become obsessed with fulfillment. Yet study Christ and His nature, being, and attributes, and you will find the God Who determines our destinies. A writer and a preacher whom Joshua and I both greatly respect and read often is the Englishman of the nineteenth century, Charles Spurgeon. The following are four important things he suggests we remember about reading. These are things to remember as you read this valuable book:

- Earnestly desire godly books.

[Speaking of Paul's words in 2 Timothy 4:13]:

He was inspired, and yet he wants books!

He had been preaching for thirty years, and yet he wants books!

He had seen the Lord, and yet he wants books!

He had a wider experience than most men do, and yet he wants books!

He had been caught up into the third heaven, and had heard things that it was not lawful for a man to utter, and yet he wants books!

He had written a major part of the New Testament, and yet he wants books!

- Renounce light literature.

"'Give yourself to reading.' . . . You need to read. Renounce as much as you will all light literature, but study as much as possible sound theological works, especially the Puritan writers, and expositions of the Bible."

- Godly books drive us to the Bible.

"Visit many good books, but live in the Bible . . . All human books grow stale after a time—but with the Word of God the desire to study it increases, while the more you know of it the less you think you know. The Book grows upon you: as you dive into its depths you have a fuller perception of the infinity which remains to be explored. You are still sighing to enjoy more of that which it is your bliss to taste.

- Read deeply more than broadly.

Master those books you have. Read them thoroughly. Bathe in them until they saturate you. Read and reread them . . . digest them. Let them go into your very self. Peruse a good book several times and make notes and analyses of it. A student will find that his mental constitution is more affected by one book thoroughly mastered than by twenty books he has merely skimmed. Little learning and much pride comes from hasty reading. Some men are disabled from thinking by their putting meditation away for the sake of much reading. In reading let your motto be 'much not many.' Give yourself unto reading. The man who never reads will never be read; he who never quotes will never be quoted. He who will not use the thoughts of other men's brains, proves that he has no brains of his own. You need to read.

Here is why I highly recommend Joshua West's book, *Come and Die*:

- It is a godly book.

- It is not light literature.

- It will drive you to the Bible.

- It can be read and reread to take you deeper into the things of God.

-Gary Wilkerson
President of World Challenge

Truly, truly, I say to you, unless a grain of wheat falls into the earth and dies, it remains alone; but if it dies, it bears much fruit. Whoever loves his life loses it, and whoever hates his life in this world will keep it for eternal life. If anyone serves me, he must follow me; and where I am, there will my servant be also. If anyone serves me, the Father will honor him.

—John 12:24-26

INTRODUCTION

Let me start by saying that this book is by no means exhaustive. Writing a book about a topic like Christian discipleship is a very daunting task. My hope is to emphasize biblical truths that I feel are left out of much of the modern writing on the subject. The purpose of this book and all of my writings is to point people toward a contextual study of the Bible, which is the exhaustive book on Christian discipleship and which points people to Jesus as revealed in Scripture.

I also hope that this simple book might create in you a hunger to dig deeper into biblical doctrine so that you build a theology that comes from Scripture and not just from what your favorite Bible teacher says. Don't get me wrong; I am very thankful for sound preachers and biblical teachers like John Piper, David Wilkerson, Paul Washer, Leonard Ravenhill, and Alistair Begg and, of course, timeless authors like Charles Spurgeon, J.C. Ryle, A.W. Tozer, and Martyn LLoyd Jones. The insight of men like these has aided me greatly in my study of the Scriptures, but it is very important to make sure it is the Scripture we hold as the highest authority, not men, as learned and wise as they might be.

Most modern books that deal with the topic of Christian discipleship seem to focus much more on man rather than God, as does much of Christianity today—what we can expect from God rather than what the sovereign God of the universe expects from us. Without being pragmatic or irreverent to Scripture, I wanted to write a book on discipleship that makes much of God and Scripture and answers practical questions Christians encounter while walking out their faith.

The Bible is God's story and His revelation to mankind. We shouldn't try to superimpose ourselves into the Scripture to make it more applicable to us. The Scripture should change us and mold our view of God, life, and ourselves, not the other way around. It can be very confusing looking for yourself in a book (the Bible) that isn't about you but, rather, is about God. We desperately need sound doctrine to once again be seen as paramount in our churches and in our lives. Many people today hate words like *doctrine* because it seems rigid and old-fashioned to them, but doctrine is what you believe and by which you live. If the Bible doesn't dictate what you believe, something else will. This book is my attempt at a Christ-centered, Gospel-rich, biblically sound entrance into Christian discipleship.

So often in American Christianity, we hear that being saved and being a disciple of Jesus are two different things. We are taught that you can make a verbal declaration of faith but never follow Jesus or live for Him. Old-time preachers call this "fire insurance." This is the idea that if you recite certain words in a church meeting and that the preacher can pronounce you as saved, you may not actually live for the Lord or follow Him, but at least you are saved and won't go to Hell. I find this nowhere in the Scripture and see it as a great stumbling block to preaching the Gospel to people because so many who are lost have the false assurance that they are saved.

Christianity is all about regeneration, which is just a theological word meaning "reborn" or "born again." When we are born again, we take on a new nature. God reorients our heart, and we are changed. Jesus makes it clear that He will spit the lukewarm from His mouth. Those who do not follow Him are not worthy of Him, and those who love Him will keep His commands. The Gospel isn't salvation through works; it is a free gift of God's grace. But if you have been reborn and your eyes have been opened to the truth, you will follow Jesus, and your life will be different—not by your power but by the power of the Spirit of Christ, Who lives within you. It is my hope you let the Scriptures bear this out throughout the pages of this book.

I have gone to great lengths to write a simple book on Christian discipleship that is biblical and sound; that will correct, rebuke, and encourage according to the Scripture; and that will bring biblical balance to the subject. I also understand that there might be secondary issues on which we might not agree, and that is okay. By secondary issues, I mean things that do not undermine the biblical Gospel, the nature of Christ, the Trinity, and other timeless, essential beliefs of Christian orthodoxy. My hope is that this book will awaken hunger and love for the Scripture within Christians at all places in their walk and that through the Scripture, the light of truth might expose deception and confusion in your life so that you can walk out your faith with biblical integrity. I also hope this book will be a bridge to some who have rejected deeper theological studies in the past and will encourage them to see that theology does matter. How we view the Scripture has much to do with how we view God and how we follow Jesus.

Finally, please remember that I am a flawed human being and know that because of that fact alone, this work is imperfect in some way. But my humble prayer is that God will use it anyway to encourage His people in the faith as Christian disciples as we die to ourselves and follow Jesus. This book is a call from Scripture to abandon your kingdom and your treasure and surrender to the King, Who is mightier than all and Whose kingdom will never pass away—a call to come and die, so that you might live.

CHAPTER 1

DON'T SKIP THE GOSPEL

"For I decided to know nothing among you except Jesus Christ and him crucified."

1 Cor 2:2

There is nothing more beautiful and powerful in this life than the love of God displayed to us in the Gospel of truth by which we are saved. But let us remember that without truth, there is no love. Love and truth are irrevocably tied to one another. They are different sides to the same coin. You can't divorce truth and love from each other any more than you can divorce truth and love from God. Believing that you can withhold the truth and be loving is like having a beautiful car without an engine. It might be nice to look at, but it can't take you anywhere and, really, is good for nothing. The truth and love of God converge in the Gospel more than anywhere else in human history. The Gospel isn't just the beginning of the Christian life; it is the Christian life.

I have been accused at times of trying to make everything I teach or preach about the Gospel. I have been called a one-dimensional preacher who always tries to make every sermon lead back to the cross. I hope that this accusation is true, and I pray that I am found guilty of this without a doubt when I stand before God one day. Everything in the church and in the life of a Christian should be centered around the Gospel of Jesus Christ, especially matters pertaining to Christian discipleship. That being said, it appears that often today, the Gospel is not a primary element in what we call Christian discipleship. Now I must be clear that I don't think most churches or pastors in the world would disagree with the statement that the Gospel must be central in discipleship, but in practice, I believe many do disagree to what they give emphasis, on what they focus, and on what they often leave out.

We tend to try and make discipleship seem more appealing by focusing on practicality or what people think they need rather than focusing on what Jesus says and on what the Bible focuses. While you might sell a lot more books that way or get better speaking invitations because of it, what gets produced will be lacking and deficient. Please understand, I'm not saying that I have a better method than the other guy. I'm only saying that we must carefully search God's Word and obey it, realizing it has all the answers we need as Christians.

Too often today, the Gospel is viewed as something we do before we enter into discipleship, but the truth is, the Gospel of Jesus Christ is the central point of all discipleship. We will never outgrow it, and we will never move past it. It's the measuring stick we continually use to check our intentions, expose our flesh, and compare ourselves to the finished work of Christ Jesus our Lord.

The atmosphere today in many churches is so centered on church growth at any cost, personal comfort, and what we want God to do for us, we often fail to push people toward the narrow path of the Gospel. That place is where our life is confronted with the message of Jesus that tells us to deny ourselves, pick up our cross, and follow Him, to lay everything down for Him and to give up complete control of our lives. You can't disciple someone to whom you are pandering, someone you are trying to entertain or impress, or someone to whom you are trying to sell something. The Gospel continually challenges us through purposeful examination to compare ourselves to Jesus—Who He is and what He demands from us as His followers. One of the biggest problems we face is that many within the Church of today treat the Gospel as if it is something we present to people once in the beginning, get them to "accept it," and then continue on to the more important things of Christianity. Teaching people that they can accept Christ without following Him has made a crisis of sorts in the area of Christian discipleship. Expecting people to live out true Christianity when they are still unconverted is not only foolish and unproductive, but it is also cruel.

The Gospel is not only the beginning of becoming a Christian; it's also the center of Christianity. The life, death, and resurrection of Jesus Christ is the lens through which we should view everything else. This is why we must preach the Gospel in its fullness and often. A church that doesn't preach about sin and final judgment isn't really preaching the Gospel. A pastor who doesn't labor to stress the exclusivity of Christ in his preaching leaves room for the people under the sound of his voice to make dangerous assumptions about Who God really is and what it truly means to be saved. The truth is, church consulting groups and church growth experts go to great lengths to encourage pastors not to be divisive, but the Gospel is divisive by nature. Its wisdom cries out over and over again the message of Jesus Himself: "Repent, for the kingdom of heaven is at hand" (Matt. 4:17). But churches seem to grow faster when you add just enough truth to draw in undiscerning Christians and leave out enough truth to comfort the conscience of the false convert and unbeliever. This creates unhealthy numerical growth in churches as well as false security for people who have not truly committed their lives to Christ.

You can fill churches with people who think they are saved, when they really are not, but you can't make them disciples because true disciples are followers of Jesus, not mere spectators. Churches are full of spectators— people who come for entertainment and encouragement, who are very interested to know what services the church provides but not very interested in being a servant and definitely not interested in being a disciple.

The Gospel cuts through all of this. Of course, we want those outside of Christ to come to our church, and yes, we want to reach out to them to draw them in, but for the sake of presenting the Gospel, not to merely fill a seat.

The Gospel is good news for a sinful and lost mankind, not an initiation into a social club. A major part of sharing the Gospel is sharing the bad news that makes the good news good. What does this mean? Without the awareness that we are all sinners headed for eternal damnation, we don't really see the work of Christ as the good news that it actually is.

A true Gospel preacher should always be dividing the room in which he is preaching. Preaching the Gospel in its fullness does this. We should always make the message clear when we are addressing Christians and when we are addressing lost people. Drawing lost people to repentance and encouraging those in Christ to keep fighting the good fight should be the focus. But even Christians need the message of repentance, and often, this helps us continually evaluate ourselves and test ourselves in light of the finished work of Jesus Christ.

Discipleship doesn't start until conversion, and many who claim Christ are not really His, which is why we must continually challenge ourselves with the words of our Savior to come and die to ourselves. Often when a new convert comes to salvation, they will keep questioning if they are saved because they are now aware of something that they were not before—sin. And as we grow in Christ, we begin to develop a disdain for sin that wasn't there before. Both Christians and non-Christians alike sin; the difference is those who have truly been regenerated hate sin, and as we continue to "bear fruit in keeping with repentance," we hate it all the more.

***

"Bear fruit in keeping with repentance."

Matt. 3:8

A preacher should not try to push people past the work of the Holy Spirit in convicting someone of sin. I think this is one reason that the high pressure/high stakes altar call produces many false converts; it might produce a profession of faith, but it produces very few disciples. Remember, we are not trying to push people into repeating a prayer; we are asking them, for the sake of Christ, to give up their entire life. And while I believe that God moves on the hearts of people to draw them to repentance during church services, I also believe that we should never dare try and produce this result on our own. The truth is, when God moves, it's not because we have the lights dimmed a certain way or because emotional keyboard music is playing. I'm not criticizing a keyboard being played or mood lighting; I'm just saying, if you think that is what causes the presence of almighty God to be tangible in a particular service, you are arrogant and deceived. When we worship God "in spirit and truth" (John 4:24), we are worshiping Him in a way that is pleasing to Him. We know this because it is biblically prescribed.

***

> Now I would remind you, brothers, of the gospel I preached to you, which you received, in which you stand, and by which you are being saved, if you hold fast to the word I preached to you—unless you believed in vain. For I delivered to you as of first importance what I also received: that Christ died for our sins in accordance with the Scriptures, that he was buried, that he was raised on the third day in accordance with the Scriptures (1 Cor. 15:1-4).

We take our stand on our profession of faith, but a true profession must be rooted in true belief. In the Gospel, we have been saved by Christ; we are being saved through Christ; and ultimately, one day, we will be saved in Christ.

Here is an imperfect analogy of salvation. If you were shipwrecked and floating on the open sea, you would be in need of a savior. If a rescue boat came out to save you, the moment they pulled you out of the water into the boat, you would be saved; and as the boat rushed you toward the shore, you are in the process of being saved. When you arrive at the safety of the shore, you would ultimately be saved. This is a crude way of explaining salvation.

Maybe this analogy is better: You are in in a car accident. You are bleeding and wounded, and your heart stops. Right about that time, an ambulance pulls up, and a paramedic jumps out and hits you with the paddles; your heart begins to beat, and you come back to life. At that moment, you are saved. Then you are put into an ambulance, and the machines sustain your heart while the paramedic works on your wounds and tries to stop the bleeding. During the ambulance ride, you are being saved. And once you arrive at the hospital and have the surgery that saves your life, you are ultimately saved.

Of course, these are just crude analogies that attempt to explain the very deep concept of how salvation is a part of our lives as Christians from the point of conversion until we are glorified in Christ upon death, but hopefully, they shed some light on the fact that salvation is something much more involved than merely repeating a prayer. One important thing to remember is that at every stage of salvation, it is God doing the saving, not us.

John Calvin said, "The gospel is not a doctrine of the tongue, but of life. It cannot be grasped by reason and memory only, but it is fully understood when it possesses the whole soul and penetrates to the inner recesses of the heart." While it's true that the Gospel isn't merely a magic prayer you say, it is also not just an exercise of reason and intellect. It does involve these things, but simply understanding the Gospel doesn't make you saved and definitely doesn't make you a follower of Jesus. Many men and women have understood the Gospel but would not let it penetrate the deep recesses of the heart, as they wrestle not with the reality of the finished work of Christ logically but for how truly desperate their need of Him is. This quote from Calvin is so very true. Salvation is not a doctrine of the tongue but of the heart. So many profess Jesus with their tongue but have no evidence to back it up. Remember the evidence is for your surety of salvation, not for God's. He knows who are His, so you can't pretend with Him or prove anything to Him. One of the greatest revelations of my life from the words of Scripture was this: God truly does know my heart, and He knows it better than I do

(Jer. 17:9). The hidden potential, the wicked intentions, the selfish ambitions, the good things, the bad things, and everything in between—He sees it all. There is no hiding from God.

***

> O Lord, you have searched me and known me! You know when I sit down and when I rise up; you discern my thoughts from afar. You search out my path and my lying down and are acquainted with all my ways. Even before a word is on my tongue, behold, O Lord, you know it altogether. You hem me in, behind and before, and lay your hand upon me. Such knowledge is too wonderful for me; it is high; I cannot attain it. Where shall I go from your Spirit? Or where shall I flee from your presence? If I ascend to heaven, you are there! If I make my bed in Sheol, you are there! If I take the wings of the morning and dwell in the uttermost parts of the sea, even there your hand shall lead me, and your right hand shall hold me. If I say, "Surely the darkness shall cover me, and the light about me be night," even the darkness is not dark to you; the night is bright as the day, for darkness is as light with you. For you formed my inward parts; you knitted me together in my mother's womb (Psalm 139:1-13).

God created us and everything else; He knows us inside and out. So, part of having faith in God is knowing that although it may not always seem like it, God is in control, and we must trust that fact. God is omniscient, which means that He is all-knowing. There isn't anything that God doesn't know. We can never preach the Gospel too much because this good news is the most important message in history; it convicts lost sinners, draws them to repentance, and encourages those who have been saved by bringing much needed surety to their salvation.

THE PURPOSE OF THE GOSPEL

Although the analogies we discussed about salvation may shed light on what salvation looks like in process, it does nothing to explain God's purpose in saving us. Why would a perfect God save wretched sinners like us? Why would God go to such great lengths to make a way for us to avoid eternal destruction? Why would God call us "out of darkness into his marvelous light" (1 Peter 2:9)? If He is calling us out of something, to what then is He calling us? One of the clearest places the Bible explains the purpose of the Gospel and why Jesus took on flesh is in the book of John. John focuses a great deal on Jesus' relationship with humanity. In John's gospel, it seems that we see the compassion and humanity of Jesus more than we do in the synoptic gospels, and from this vantage point, I believe we see God's purpose in salvation for humanity more than elsewhere in the New Testament.

***

"But to all who did receive him, who believed in his name, he gave the right to become children of God, who were born, not of blood nor of the will of the flesh nor of the will of man, but of God."

John 1:12-13

It seems that God has set us apart in salvation to be called His sons and daughters. This is amazing! The reason God saved us was to bring glory to His name by making us His children. This is a mind-blowing concept. Just read the first several chapters of Romans, and we are made painfully aware that we are all sinners and that no one in humanity is good because "all have sinned and fall short of the glory of God" (Rom. 3:23). The due penalty for all sin is death. We deserve death—all of us—and it is in light of this fact that God presents the gift of His grace in the Gospel.

***

"For the wages of sin is death, but the free gift of God is eternal life in Christ Jesus our Lord."

Rom. 6:23

Salvation is a gift, and what an amazing gift it is. God chose to make us His sons and daughters through the transforming power of the Gospel. But as reborn children of God, we must still also be God's willing servants and disciples—not because we deserve it, but merely because it is His will to have us in His family. There are certain aspects to the mystery of God's love I am convinced we are incapable of understanding as humans. Maybe in the age to come we will be able to understand it more clearly, but it is not necessary that we completely understand it, only that we repent and accept it. Every day, we are truly in a relationship with God, so we have the opportunity to grow in the knowledge of His love.

Part of this mystery is the actual miracle of being reborn into this family. We live a blind and dark life of sin, unaware of true love, joy, and peace. Then suddenly, but not all at once, we see a light that has always been there but was unknown to us before. The only good explanation of this is when we were born. When a baby is born, everything is new. We must learn how to do everything—eat, walk, talk, and reason. There was nothing before, and suddenly, one day, life begins. Just think about everything that happens once a baby is born and all the human things he or she must learn in a lifetime. But nothing can begin until the baby is actually born. We can't teach him or her anything until that amazing day the mother goes into labor and the baby joins us in the land of the living.

One reason this is so challenging for us to see is because we have been living this sort of sub-life as sinners. We have learned and adapted to life over our years on this planet, but everything we know is corrupted by sin, not just outward sin we are exposed to but also the inward sin with which we are born. We think we know love, but we don't; we think we understand what being at peace is, but it's not real peace; we think we understand what happiness and joy are, but until we are regenerated and reborn through Christ, we are truly incapable of experiencing these things in any real way. But you think you do because your experience in life is your only frame of reference.

In the third chapter of John, Jesus explains this mystery to a Pharisee named Nicodemus, who was a member of the Jewish ruling council.

Nicodemus seemed to be convinced that Jesus was some sort of prophet due to the signs He was performing but still didn't really understand that Jesus was truly the Messiah. I believe this might have been why he met Jesus to discuss these things in the night and not during the daytime.

> Now there was a man of the Pharisees named Nicodemus, a ruler of the Jews. This man came to Jesus by night and said to him, "Rabbi, we know that you are a teacher come from God, for no one can do these signs that you do unless God is with him." Jesus answered him, "Truly, truly, I say to you, unless one is born again he cannot see the kingdom of God." Nicodemus said to him, "How can a man be born when he is old? Can he enter a second time into his mother's womb and be born?" Jesus answered, "Truly, truly, I say to you, unless one is born of water and the Spirit, he cannot enter the kingdom of God. That which is born of the flesh is flesh, and that which is born of the Spirit is spirit. Do not marvel that I said to you, 'You must be born again.' The wind blows where it wishes, and you hear its sound, but you do not know where it comes from or where it goes. So it is with everyone who is born of the Spirit" (John 3:1-8).

In the Gospel, we are reborn into God's family and take on a new nature. This is a miraculous gift from God. Nothing we could ever do could produce a new life in the Spirit. Regeneration is the gift of salvation, and Christian discipleship is the growth and conditioning process of this new life that we have been given in Christ. No one can enter the kingdom of Heaven unless they are born of water and the Spirit. We were born initially only in the corrupt fallen body of flesh, but to be part of God's family, we must be reborn in the Spirit.

One reason I believe that it is very important we preach the true and full Gospel in our churches and that we do it often is because there are so many who, like the Pharisee Nicodemus, believe they know Who God is and that they are part of His family but haven't really been reborn in the Spirit. The

Gospel is a glimpse of the Light in which we find life through the Person of Jesus Christ.

***

"In him was life, and the life was the light of men. The light shines in the darkness, and the darkness has not overcome it."

John 1:4-5

Before we can be His disciples, we must see the essential need for the miracle of spiritual rebirth into Christ to be a part of His kingdom. Christian discipleship is all about spiritual growth and conditioning, so before we can start learning or growing in the Spirit, we must be born of the Spirit. You can't be a disciple of a spiritual kingdom if you are not a reborn, spiritual being. This brings us back to the sinful human perception of things like love, peace, and joy. God's motives are very hard for us to grasp because although we are not utterly wicked—by which I mean incapable of any good—there isn't a part of our human nature that isn't touched and corrupted by sin. God is holy, pure, and altogether good, so the sacrificial nature of God's perfect love is very hard for selfish humans to perceive. But it is in the perception and acceptance of this love that we find transformation in every other area of our life. We will discuss this in greater detail in a later chapter of this book.

***

"For God so loved the world, that he gave his only Son, that whoever believes in him should not perish but have eternal life. For God did not send his Son into the world to condemn the world, but in order that the world might be saved through him. Whoever believes in him is not condemned, but whoever does not believe is condemned already, because he has not believed in the name of the only Son of God. And this is the judgment: the light has come into the world, and people loved the darkness rather than the light because their works were evil. For everyone who does wicked things hates the light and does not come to the light, lest his works should be exposed.

*But whoever does what is true comes to the light, so that it may be clearly
seen that his works have been carried out in God."*

John 3:16-21

John 3:16-17 is quoted often but can be easily misrepresented if understood apart from verses eighteen through twenty-one. It was God's love for us that set the work of the cross in motion. In God's sovereignty, the cross was always part of the plan of redemption. God didn't send His Son to condemn us because, as the Scripture makes clear, without Him, we already stand condemned. We are born in darkness, and those who love darkness will stay there because they love sin and don't want their deeds to be exposed. The truth of the Gospel is the light of God in a dark and sinful world inviting us to come out of darkness and expose our deeds in repentance. This is what it means to accept the love of God into your life. You cannot divorce the truth of God and the love of God. The light of the Gospel that draws us to repentance is the beginning of Christian discipleship.

The purpose of our creation, redemption, sanctification, and glorification is found in the love of God, which serves ultimately to glorify God because God is love. God's love displayed for us on the cross is a glimpse into the eternal love of the Trinity and the means by which we are saved and included in God's family somehow. We could never focus on the Gospel too much because false converts will always be among us who desperately need to hear it, but that's not the only reason why. Christianity isn't a moral betterment plan for your flesh and sin nature; it is a spiritual rebirth and development plan for a new nature. True Christians also need to hear the Gospel often as well because it constantly reminds us of and redirects us toward the narrow path that leads us toward life. The Gospel should be an essential part of the life of every Christian disciple. The cross by which we were saved should be the focus and standard of the Christian life because it gives us new life in Christ and the power we need to live it.

CHAPTER 2
THE PURSUIT OF HAPPINESS

"The hope of the righteous brings joy, but the expectation of the wicked will perish."

Prov. 10:28

The greatest aim in the lives of most people is to be happy. This is what we think we are chasing when we chase anything in this life—relationships, careers, hopes, and dreams. We do this in an effort to arrive at a place we call happiness. What is ironic is that we are pursuing the wrong thing for something that we really don't even understand. The root of the word *happiness* comes from the word *happenings*. Simply put, happiness is a state of bliss that is greatly determined by what is happening in your life or your current situation. If the situation that made you feel good changes so does your state of being emotionally. Essentially, we are pursuing something that could never deliver what we hope it will.

***

"We are half-hearted creatures, fooling about with drink and sex and ambition when infinite joy is offered us, like an ignorant child who wants to go on making mud pies in a slum because he cannot imagine what is meant by the offer of a holiday at the sea. We are far too easily pleased."

—C.S. Lewis

Because this is all we know, we live for happiness wherever it can be found; and like animals, we feed on it until it's gone and begin to search for the next

31

relationship, project, or purpose we hope will hold our attention and fill our hearts. But the truth is that there is no true and lasting joy, fulfillment, and purpose in this life outside of Christ. For the unregenerate person, these words seem thin and shallow because for most people, Christ is a concept of morality or a myth. Many people who identify as Christians also find this statement lacking because they don't really know Him. I believe that it is impossible to truly have a real and personal fellowship with Christ and not see Him as all-sufficient.

So many people who call themselves Christian in today's culture scoff at this idea of the all-sufficiency of Christ. When it comes to pain and suffering and the problem of evil in the world, or when it comes to dealing with tough social issues, many people are enraged when you say Christ is enough. They honestly don't know that to be true. Much of our church culture is fixated on the here and now rather than on eternity. The idea of suffering for righteousness' sake is a foreign and bizarre concept. But honestly, you cannot read through the Bible without being confronted with this concept. This is the model and pattern of Christ Himself. Now most people in theory believe that Christ is sufficient to forgive their sins and get them to Heaven, but often, it doesn't seem to impact the state of their lives as much as temporal things do. We believe Christ saved us, but that's for later. To be happy in this life, we believe we need lots of stuff and entertainment and money and everything to go our way, and when it doesn't, we are depressed and defeated.

Christianity is often represented as moralism, which is a list of behaviors and practices that we believe make us good people. For society, this often seems like a good thing because people who are outwardly living out biblical principles often treat people better and are better for society as a whole. This is not the Gospel, though. Many people who try to live out morality may benefit the people around them somewhat, but it is not the aim of true discipleship. Getting people to do a list of things they don't want to do and, in turn, resisting things that they do want to do isn't the point of true Christianity. Christianity is about transformation, a reorientation of who you are at the heart level. As you grow in sanctification, your desires begin to change. There is also a supernatural renewal of your mind that comes from the study of God's Word and prayer. Here is a principle that I have found to be true over my years serving the Lord: as we grow in sanctification in the Lord, we grow in satisfaction in the Lord.

So, being a Christian doesn't mean you only do things that make you unhappy; it also means the things that make you happy begin to change. But ultimately, happiness is a small, emotional puddle that eventually gets swallowed up in the sea of something so much greater and deeper than any type of temporary human happiness. Joy is something that this world cannot give you and something this world cannot take away from you. If your circumstances rob you of joy, it wasn't joy to start with. This doesn't mean you are above feeling human emotions. Human emotion is part of what makes this life beautiful and so very fragile. It is completely possible to mourn deeply for the loss of someone you love and still be full of joy. Like love, joy isn't an emotion. It is part of the fruit of the Spirit. Real joy is a God-given gift, and it brings us strength.

***

"But the fruit of the Spirit is love, joy, peace, patience, kindness, goodness, faithfulness, gentleness, self-control; against such things there is no law. And those who belong to Christ Jesus have crucified the flesh with its passions and desires."

Gal. 5:22-24

Many people point their lives to end up at the location they believe will bring happiness. And when they arrive there, they realize it was a mirage. As disciples of Jesus, we find a wellspring of eternal joy in the same place we find unfailing love—in our communion with Christ Himself. The fruit of the Spirit isn't a list of character attributes to which we aspire. They are evidence of one fruit, namely that we are truly connected to the source of life and that we have crucified our flesh and worldly desires, leaving them to die.

It is impossible to be filled with real joy until we have been transformed by the love of God, specifically the love of God in the Gospel. It is in response to this love that we live our lives. It's only those who have been transformed by the love of God and who have died to the flesh that have real joy and true peace in this life. I personally believe the degree to which we die to our flesh and this world greatly determines our ability to bear spiritual fruit. A spiritual man who searches for fulfillment in temporal and worldly things is like a man who thinks he can be refreshed by drinking vinegar. He thinks if he just drinks a little more, it will eventually satisfy, but it never will. There isn't anything of the flesh that will ever bring you joy.

MORE ON JOY

"You make known to me the path of life; in your presence there is fullness of joy; at your right hand are pleasures forevermore."

Psalm 16:11

We must remember that joy is not an emotion, and true joy isn't dependent on your circumstances. We draw joy from the Spirit of God, and this joy increases as we are in His presence and as we grow in His image and likeness. This life is filled with ups and downs, and in it, we will experience many different things, both good and bad. But as Christians, we rest in the truth that this life is but a temporary affliction, and in a moment, we will be in the eternal bliss of glorification and unification with our Lord and Savior Jesus Christ. We find much joy in this truth; and if truly believed, it will see us through any and every trial. But another source of great joy in this life is living a life that brings God glory and draws men to Christ. Our lives do not belong to us; they belong to the Lord. They are for His glory and His purposes. Many today in Christian culture believe God saved us for our glory and that God only glories when we have everything our worldly heart desires. This is why so many fall victim to the lie of the prosperity gospel. The prosperity gospel promotes the idea that God is only glorified if we are financially rich and physically healthy. It tells you that you can have God and everything else you want in life, but honestly, you have to really twist the Scripture to believe this lie. Yet many believe it because they so desperately want it to be true.

The life of Jesus and the apostles show us something much different than this, and through their lives and what they taught, we see the beauty of suffering and sacrifice. Paul lived a very hard life by most accounts, and yet no one in the New Testament talks more about rejoicing in the Lord than he. As long as we try to find happiness in worldly things, we will always be let down because happiness can disappear in a moment. Here is an idea most people reject but that is nonetheless true: life is not about pursuing personal happiness. Life is about pursuing God and worshiping Him "in Spirit and in truth" (John 4:24), bringing Him glory in all that we do. For those of us who are truly in Christ, there is no greater joy and satisfaction in life than this.

***

*"Though you have not seen him, you love him. Though you do not now
see him, you believe in him and rejoice with joy that is inexpressible and
filled with glory, obtaining the outcome of your faith,
the salvation of your souls."*

1 Peter 1:8-9

It is this very faith that produces unquenchable joy in our hearts. Many claim to have this saving faith but seem hopeless and joyless. If "to live is Christ, and to die is gain," as Philippians 1:22 says, how could a true believer be hopeless? You might be discouraged, depressed, tired, weak, or frustrated, but hopeless never. How could things in your life and in this world make you hopeless when, as a Christian, your hope is rooted in something outside of this life and outside of this world? Often, people are so consumed with the love of this world and the things in this world that when their circumstances change, they are shattered. All things in this life fade—youth, beauty, health, money—all are passing away and quickly. Tying our hope to any temporal thing is a fool's errand. As the children of God, we should be filled with an inexpressible and glorious joy that transcends our circumstances in this life because we know that as this life fades, we are moving closer to receiving the end result of our faith—the salvation of our souls. So, if you are not filled with joy and gratefulness about the salvation of your soul, especially as you get closer to it, my question is why not?

Some Christians' capacity to experience joy has been greatly diminished due to mass consumption of worldly garbage. It's just like when you were a kid and you ate a bunch of candy and junk food before dinner. Even if your mother made your favorite meal, you weren't really hungry for it. You were full, but you weren't satisfied; and your stomach ached. But because you were an immature child, you would do it again if given the chance. Everywhere you look in our culture, there is spiritual candy and junk food, some of it not very good for you and some of it flat out bad for you. It never satisfies our hunger or nourishes our body, but because it's sweet and delicious, we fill ourselves with it. We want instant gratification and constant stimulation to the point that when we don't get it, we become depressed. We are so overloaded with junk, we aren't very hungry for real spiritual food. And because our spirits are not being nourished, we are sick and weak.

Self-denial isn't salvation by works, and it isn't legalism. Denying ourselves of things that separate us from God and pollute our spirits isn't legalism; it's just logical. Christ is the Source of life and our joy; and as we revel in His glory, in His Word, and in prayer and worship, we become healthy and strong disciples. We need a consistent diet of these things, and we must resist and cut out things that subdue us into complacency.

***

"And let the peace of Christ rule in your hearts,
to which indeed you were called in one body. And be thankful."

Col. 3:15

As most pursue happiness in this life, we also hope that when we find this happiness, we will also find peace. It is very ironic to me that as we look across the landscape of our culture and the world, everyone seems to be pursuing all the things that can only be found in Christ, but it seems that most would rather do nearly anything else than accept this truth. The problem is that many look for an external peace when what they really need is an internal peace. Some do look inward but end up realizing that the answer isn't inside of them either. The truth is that we need an internal peace that comes from an external source. Because of sin, we are corrupted and disconnected from the Source to which we were designed to be connected. This peace is something beyond our human understanding and out of human reach.

***

Do not be anxious about anything, but in everything by prayer and supplication with thanksgiving let your requests be made known to God. And the peace of God, which surpasses all understanding, will guard your hearts and your minds in Christ Jesus. Finally, brothers, whatever is true, whatever is honorable, whatever is just, whatever is pure, whatever is lovely, whatever is commendable, if there is any excellence, if there is anything worthy of praise, think about these things.

Phil. 4:6-8

The peace of God is the only thing that can fill our empty hearts. Being at peace with our Maker is to be alive in Christ. We will never have true peace in our hearts and in our lives until we have "the peace of God, which surpasses all understanding." This doesn't mean we Christians don't use reason, but the peace that comes from God in knowing our sin is forgiven and that we belong to God brings a peace that envelops our lives and transcends our reason. Trying to use God to get what we need from Him isn't the point. The point and purpose of this life is to find our worth, value, and fulfillment in one solitary thing—Christ alone. The only way to have real life is to lose your life for the purposes of God. This is where we find hope, and this is where we find our joy. In Him, we are filled with an internal peace that is beyond human understanding. We were designed to bring glory to our Creator. A life that is full of everything else but Him lacks everything.

***

"For whoever would save his life will lose it,
but whoever loses his life for my sake will find it."

Matt. 16:25

The only way to really ever be happy in this life is to let go of everything. The only way to find a real life with purpose and fulfillment is to completely abandon your old life in exchange for a life fully rooted in Christ as revealed in Scripture. Joy and peace are something that come together because they are part of the same fruit of the same Spirit. God never promised that our life or our circumstances would be peaceful or easy; in fact, He told us the opposite of that. What Christ *did* say was that if our hope, joy, and peace are found in the fact that He overcame the world, we would also overcome the world through Him: "I have said these things to you, that in me you may have peace. In the world you will have tribulation. But take heart; I have overcome the world" (John 16:33).

So why is it, then, that we see so many Christians who say they believe this, but their lives say something different? Honestly, most of the time, it's fairly obvious that you can't overcome a world that you still love, by which you still want to be accepted and approved, and of which you are unwilling to let go. There really is no middle ground; it's follow God or the world, love God or the world. "For where your treasure is, there your heart will be also" (Matt. 6:21).

JOY AND GRATEFULNESS

Joy and gratefulness are two things that are eternally connected and inseparable. Gratefulness is the byproduct and evidence of someone who is truly filled with the joy of the Lord. True thanksgiving comes from the understanding that we were rebel sinners scheduled for damnation, but because of what Christ has done for us, we Christians have been pardoned from Hell and have been adopted into the family of God. Knowing this at the heart level will change everything about your life. If your hope is tied up in salvation through Christ and the promise of a future reward that is beyond comparison to anything in this life, then gratefulness and thanksgiving is just evidence that you really believe it. It is evidence of your transformation.

Many people in this life claim to know Christ in this way but are still ungrateful and unthankful when they believe life is hard or unfair. I believe gratitude is like a thermometer by which we can judge the condition of our hearts as Christians. We can't judge our walk with God based on the circumstances that surround us. Many people pursue wealth and worldly success and believe because they achieve it that they are blessed by God. But take all of their success away, and they become bitter and upset. Show me a person who is full of joy, contentment, and gratitude in either circumstance, and I'll show you a person whose heart is rooted in Christ.

***

"I know how to be brought low, and I know how to abound. In any and every circumstance, I have learned the secret of facing plenty and hunger, abundance and need. I can do all things through him who strengthens me."

Phil. 4:12-13

The apostle Paul wasn't perfect, and through His writings, we see that even he became discouraged at times. He writes that sometimes he felt abandoned and forgotten, but these are a few passing statements, not the bulk of his writing. And even in those times, he was still filled with thanksgiving and joy. He drew his hope and his strength from Christ. This is a supernatural strength that this world can't give you and can't take away.

When you read the first chapter of Paul's epistle to the Philippians, it is hard to believe he is writing this letter from prison. He is full of thanksgiving and gratefulness for the opportunity to use this experience to forward the Gospel and to suffer for the name of Jesus. The only concerns he seems to have are for his brothers and sisters in Christ at the church in Philippi, not for himself or his own well-being. He is a man filled with the joy of the Lord, which is expressed in gratitude and is magnified by the fact that he is in chains and in prison. He was joyful and even grateful that these extreme circumstances showcased the fact that his joy was rooted in a future destination and a future reward, and he proved this by living it out until the day he was martyred.

The lives of Jesus and the apostles were obviously not spent in pursuit of comfort or happiness in this life. If we are really following Jesus like the apostles, neither should ours. If you are pursuing happiness outside of Christ, it's probably because your life is not rooted in Him, or at the very least, your relationship with Him is shallow and superficial. The answer for the unsatisfied life is Christ. The only true fulfillment in this life is found in Christ. In Him are deep rivers of joy and unwavering peace. Pursuit of happiness is wasted time and, in the end, will be the ultimate waste of your life. Pursuing happiness is like trying to take hold of the wind with your hands. Although it's there and you can feel it pass by you, it was never meant to hold you or be held by you.

In the end, you can only pursue one thing. Although our hope, joy, and peace come from God, these are not the things we disciples are pursuing; it is God Himself. To know God and be known by Him is the aim of the true follower of Christ. Thinking we can pursue happiness and God at the same time is a lie that self-deceived people tell themselves to soothe their consciences as they chase things other than Christ. You can enjoy other things along the way, but don't be deceived. You can only pursue one thing in this life, and what you choose determines your destiny and eternity.

CHAPTER 3
CONFORMING TO HIS IMAGE

"And we all, with unveiled face, beholding the glory of the Lord, are being
transformed into the same image from one degree of glory to another.
For this comes from the Lord who is the Spirit."

2 Cor. 3:18

Christian discipleship doesn't start with the idea that we should work at self-improvement to be better people. It starts with the supernatural idea that we have literally taken on a new nature in Christ. The Bible tells us that we are made in the very image of God, but in the Fall, mankind became separated from Him. Every person born after the Fall of mankind is not only born into the curse that Adam and Eve caused when they sinned but also are born enemies of God. Romans 5:10 says, "For if while we were enemies we were reconciled to God by the death of his Son, much more, now that we are reconciled, shall we be saved by his life."

This is why the Gospel is so paramount in Christian discipleship—because it is through what Christ accomplished on the cross that we are saved from the destruction that will befall all of God's enemies. Understanding who we were before Christ helps us see with the proper perspective how desperately we need Him and how unqualified and utterly unable we are to change ourselves.

In the *Merriam-Webster* dictionary, the word *disciple* means, "One who accepts and assists in teaching the doctrine of another."[1] *Discipline* comes from *disciple*, the Latin word for *pupil*, which also provided the source of the word. Being a disciple has a lot to do with discipline. This concept makes perfect sense to us when we are talking about any other area of personal growth, but for some reason, many reject it when it comes to being a Christian.

Many of us have been taught that being saved by grace means that any form of effort on your part amounts to legalistic works and should be rejected, but this simply isn't true. Now, please don't misunderstand me; I am not saying our works have anything to do with salvation. Salvation is a gift given by the grace of God alone, through faith in Christ alone (Eph. 2:8-9). I am not talking about you adding to your salvation or even that you can cause yourself to grow. I am simply saying that the Bible tells us to deny ourselves and follow Jesus—not simply walking after Him but striving to be like Him in every area of our lives. This is impossible to achieve without the power of the Holy Spirit. God has a way of life He commands us to live, but He also provides the power through His Spirit to live it out.

Being a disciple means to live a life as prescribed by the teaching of the teacher. Being a disciple of Jesus isn't an event; it is a lifelong conditioning process. In Christian theology, we call this process "sanctification." Sanctification is a lifelong process in which we are set apart from the world for God's holy use. In sanctification, we are being purified from the stain of sin and are being conformed to the very image of the One Who is purifying and saving us, Christ Jesus. The Bible compares our lives to a vase being made on a potter's wheel or gold that is refined by fire as it is repeatedly put into the flame, each time removing a little more impurity, a process that is repeated over and over again until no impurity is left. Sanctification is working sin and impurity out of our lives until the day we die and are made perfect in glorification.

---

1   *Merriam-Webster, s.v.* "Disciple," accessed March 24, 2021, https://www.merriam-webster.com/dictionary/disciple.

When talking about the conditioning of the Christian life, it's hard to find a better example than an Olympic athlete. People who compete at this level are very disciplined disciples of their craft. They don't just show up and compete; they live it. Every part of their life becomes consumed and affected by their goal—to win their event. From a very young age, most begin training with daily exercise and strict dieting. They give up a lot of pleasures that other people enjoy because their life is fixated on one thing: winning a gold medal. The coach tells them to run, and they run; the coach tells them to do drills, and they do drills; the coach prescribes a particular diet, and they must abide by it. The athlete must trust that their coach and trainers know what they are talking about because they are experts and have experience and proven success. But none of the diets, training, and practice matter if the athlete doesn't do it.

Following Christ means that we die to an old life and take on an entirely new life. The Christian life is a life of discipline and sacrifice, but like the Olympic athlete, we are motivated by what the Scripture tells us is the prize: being free from sin and spending eternity in the presence of our Lord. Christ is the Reward.

This is where the trouble starts for many people. They are striving toward something they don't actually see as worthy. If we don't see Christ Himself as worthy of what we lay down in this life, we don't really see Christ at all. Christ is worthy of all the praise, worship, and adoration we could ever bestow on Him, and He is worth abandoning everything else. The apostle Paul uses this same familiar imagery in his first letter to the Corinthians as he explains the dedication it takes to be a follower of Christ and what it takes to achieve the prize:

> Do you not know that in a race all the runners run, but only one receives the prize? So run that you may obtain it. Every athlete exercises self-control in all things. They do it to receive a perishable wreath, but we an imperishable. So I do not run aimlessly; I do

not box as one beating the air. But I discipline my body and keep it under control, lest after preaching to others I myself should be disqualified (1 Cor. 9:24-27).

All other treasures fade and pale in comparison to the eternal beauty of our Savior Jesus. He deserves all the glory and honor we can bestow on Him. This is why making the Gospel about anything other than Christ alone is so disgraceful. So, as we are made alive in Christ in salvation, we begin to conform to His image day by day through sanctification.

We tend to underestimate how dire our circumstances were outside of Christ, and because of this, we are often perplexed as Christians when we don't easily break free from our sinful nature. We are in a lose/lose situation; we have a wicked heart dead in sin that is governed by a debased and corrupt mind. So, until our heart is transformed, we have no hope. Many times, we doubt God's ability to change the minds of men because we forget that the very nature of the Gospel itself is supernatural. If we think of salvation as anything short of a resurrection, we devalue what Christ has done for us.

***

And you were dead in the trespasses and sins in which you once walked, following the course of this world, following the prince of the power of the air, the spirit that is now at work in the sons of disobedience— among whom we all once lived in the passions of our flesh, carrying out the desires of the body and the mind, and were by nature children of wrath, like the rest of mankind. But God, being rich in mercy, because of the great love with which he loved us, even when we were dead in our trespasses, made us alive together with Christ—by grace you have been saved—and raised us up with him and seated us with him in the heavenly places in Christ Jesus, so that in the coming ages he might show the immeasurable riches of his grace in kindness toward us in Christ Jesus. For by grace you have been saved through faith. And this is not your own doing; it is the gift of God, not a result of works, so that no one may boast. For we are his workmanship, created in Christ Jesus for good works, which God prepared beforehand, that we should walk in them (Eph. 2:1-10).

Most of us tend to think that although we have some shortcomings and make mistakes, deep down, we are mostly good people. When we make mistakes or do wicked things, we always like to appeal to our supposed "good intentions" or our heart. We say things like, "I'm not perfect, but God knows my heart." And we think this somehow excuses us. If you honestly thought about that statement and what it really means, you would be terrified. God really does know your heart—the wickedness, immorality, and selfish ambition; the things you would be horrified to have another human know about you, God knows.

***

"The heart is deceitful above all things, and desperately sick:
who can understand it?"

Jer. 17:9

Isn't it funny that we are often more afraid of humans finding out who we really are than the God Who will one day judge us and find us guilty based on even just one sin, let alone a lifetime of sin? Maybe it's because we don't really know God enough to fear Him, or we are so self-deceived that we think we can fool God like we think we fool everyone else. Before we can worry about the state of our mind, we must first get a brand-new heart. In salvation, God changes our heart and gives it a new nature. This is completely a gift from God and has nothing to do with self-betterment in any way, so there is nothing to boast about. Because of this gift we received as Christians, we should be known for our humility. If we have the proper perspective about the gift of salvation which we as Christians have been given by God, we should have a very hard time being prideful toward those outside of Christ.

This new heart is the very life given to us by Christ Himself; this is the life secured for us on the cross. So, we have a new heart, but unfortunately, it is still governed by a corrupt mind. This is where a lot of discipleship happens throughout the course of the Christian life; it can also be the source of a great deal of frustration. No place is our weakness more apparent than in the struggle between the mind and the spirit.

I am a graduate of a ministry called Adult and Teen Challenge. I also have the immense honor today of being the pastor and program manager at Sonrise Adult and Teen Challenge in Cache, Oklahoma. This worldwide ministry is dedicated to helping men and women with life-controlling problems overcome addiction through the transforming power of the Gospel of Jesus Christ and through intense Christian discipleship. Our center is for adult males, and it is very hard but also very rewarding work. Often when men come to us, they are gripped with addiction to drugs or alcohol and, in all honesty, are to some degree fighting against us as we are trying to help them. Some want change but don't know how to achieve it, while many simply are not ready and willing to do what it takes.

For many of them, somewhere along the way—after being constantly directed toward the narrow path of the Gospel over and over again—the light comes on, and God breathes His life into their dead and lifeless hearts. They experience the love God poured out from the cross, and they have their first taste of the joy and peace that can only come from God. They feel truly alive for the first time. Then they begin to come to the painful realization that something is still wrong. Although they have a new heart that desires new things, they still have a flesh to which they have sowed, often for many years, and a mind that has been conformed to the pattern of this fallen world. Romans 12:1-2 says:

> I appeal to you therefore, brothers, by the mercies of God, to present your bodies as a living sacrifice, holy and acceptable to God, which is your spiritual worship. Do not be conformed to this

world, but be transformed by the renewal of your mind, that by testing you may discern what is the will of God, what is good and acceptable and perfect.

Remember earlier when we used the example of the Olympic athlete, we discussed the idea of sacrificing for the sake of the sport. Here Paul is explaining that in view of the Gospel, through which God displayed so much mercy toward us, we should live our lives going forward as a living sacrifice or offering to Him. When people act like sacrificing their whole life for Christ is too much, it shows that they do not really understand the mercy God has shown to us because if they did, they would be grateful to do it. Paul says this is our true and proper worship. Paul is saying that if you really understand the sacrifice God made for us, then by comparison, what God asks from us is pretty basic.

So now we have a new heart but an unrenewed mind, and because of this, we have a hard time understanding God's will and ways. The Bible says if we want to know what God's good, pleasing, and perfect will is (Rom. 12:1-2), we must renew our mind. The question is, how do we do this? This can only be accomplished through revelation, and the most important and valuable revelation of God we have as Christians is the Scripture. Here is where things get convoluted. Many Christians believe that they are people of the Bible when they actually are not. Oftentimes, we know bits and pieces of the Scripture from teachers we follow, but we really must be students of the Bible for ourselves. Teachers and pastors are very important, but we must be students of the Bible so that we can "rightly [handle] the word of truth" (2 Tim. 2:15).

READ YOUR BIBLE AND PRAY

This seems much too simple, but the true lifeblood of a Christian is consistent reading and studying of God's Word as well as a deep and meaningful prayer life. As humans, we don't believe growing in the image of Christ is so simple. Notice I said simple, not easy. We always want an external method with quick results, like a diet pill or a financial plan that guarantees wealth overnight. The Scripture says that God has given us everything we need "for life and godliness" (2 Peter 1:3), but many Christians look elsewhere because there are many voices in our culture and in the world saying otherwise. There is nothing more important in the life of a Christian than studying the Bible daily and living a rich and full prayer life.

Although a lot of people read the Bible, it seems many would rather read books about the Bible than actually read and study the Bible itself. I'm not saying that reading Christian books is wrong; otherwise, I would be a hypocrite in writing this book. I am saying that reading Christian books is no replacement for reading the Bible itself. There is nothing wrong with books that help illuminate God's Word to us, that encourage us in the faith, and that articulate doctrines and bring clarity to hard-to-understand passages of Scripture. Christian books are great. I am an avid reader and have learned much about the faith by reading men like Martyn Lloyd Jones, A.W. Tozer, and Charles Spurgeon. But we must remember that no matter how educated and sound in the faith someone may seem, they are still fallible and subject to error. Anything we read in a book or hear from a pulpit that cannot be reconciled to the Scripture must be rejected. It is through this surrender to His Word that God begins to renew our mind. Human wisdom could never compare to the wisdom of God's Word. This is why I'm convinced that people who claim to be in Christ but do not hold to the inerrancy of Scripture may not be saved because if God is incapable of preserving the Word He said is true, then how can we trust anything God claims?

Many people want what they believe God offers them, but when they come to a passage of Scripture that is contrary to what they believe is right or good, they reject it. My question is this: if we already know what is right and good intuitively, then why do we need Scripture? Or if we trust ourselves more than we do the very words of God, then how could we ever call Him Savior and Lord?

I believe one reason is that we have reduced Christ to being the Savior of our marriages, or the One Who saves us from poverty, or the Savior of our failed plans, rather than the One Who saves us from our corrupt nature, sin, and ultimate damnation. If the Bible is true, then we cannot trust our minds, our intuition, or our human concepts about right and wrong. If the Bible is true, then we are image-bearers of God but are fallen and sinful by nature. We are God's enemies and destined for eternal punishment and damnation, but through the substitutionary death of Christ, we are afforded salvation through grace by faith in Him alone. So, this being said, if we needed God to be saved, how much more do we need Him in sanctification as we conform to the image of His Son and to walk out our faith? It is in the Scripture that we see the character of God throughout history and His wrath and His love in the Gospel. It is in the Scripture we learn how to walk out our faith and discover what is acceptable worship in the sight of God.

***

"If you love me, you will keep my commandments."

John 14:15

So, if God's Word is perfect and His greatest means of revelation to us, then shouldn't it be our greatest mission in life to study it, understand it, and use it as the scale by which we measure all knowledge? Not simply to pursue knowledge but so that we might know God from direct revelation. If something you believe does not reconcile to the Bible, it's not the Bible that's wrong; it's you. People will claim that it's not about studying the Bible but about relationship, but if you think you can have a real and meaningful relationship with God without knowing Him from Scripture, you are deceived. This is the exit ramp many young Christians take that leads them far away from true Christian discipleship. If not corrected, it will definitely lead to heresy and often will lead to apostasy. People who think they love Jesus but reject His Word don't actually love Him; they love themselves. When you reject His Word, you reject Him and instead are following your own desires.

***

"For the word of God is living and active, sharper than any two-edged sword, piercing to the division of soul and of spirit, of joints and of marrow, and discerning the thoughts and intentions of the heart."

Heb. 4:12

So how should we read and study the Bible? The same way we should read and study everything—in context. Most misuse and confusion about the Bible comes from people not reading the Scripture in context. We must understand the Bible to mean what the writer meant when they wrote it to the original audience. If you think that you can mine the Bible for deep spiritual truths without understanding it in context, you are very wrong. This is how heresy is born and cults are started. When we read the Bible, we understand that it is literal and historical, and although it was written by forty or so human authors over the span of fifteen hundred or so years, it is really written by just one author, the Holy Spirit.

God uses the Scripture to conform us to the image of Christ by dividing the soul and the spirit. It opens our eyes to the difference between what our flesh says is right and what the Spirit of God says is true. The Bible is an anchor to which we cling so that we will not be lost in the sea of human ideas. God's Word is alive and will work in our lives to make us into who God wants us to be. We should discipline ourselves to read God's Word daily. Just as our flesh needs to eat food every day or we will get weak and die, the same goes for the spiritual food of God's Word. How can we expect to be strong Christians when our diet of the Word is anorexic?

***

"But he answered, 'It is written,' Man shall not live by bread alone, but by every word that comes from the mouth of God.'"

Matt. 4:4

The Scripture is our source of life and nourishment, and it is the most important part of your life as a Christian, along with prayer. The importance of the Bible has been minimized by many claiming to be preachers and teachers, but it is paramount to the growth and discipleship of all Christians. Because of this, many people in churches are deceived today simply because they are not students of the Bible. As a pastor, I don't want to make followers for myself; I want to make followers of Jesus. My greatest desire as a pastor isn't for people to look to me but to teach them to look to God in all things— to see them saved because of the power of the Gospel, to help them establish roots and spiritual discipline that will help them grow, and, ultimately, to have them be true students of God's Word and followers of Jesus so that they can live lives of victory as they go forth and fulfill the Great Commission.

If the Bible conforms us to the image of Christ and teaches us how to live godly lives, then prayer gives us the power to do it. If we truly believe that through the Gospel of Jesus Christ, we have been given the right to approach God, then prayer should be a major part of our lives. The God Who created the universe and maintains it effortlessly has given us the privilege of communication with Him, so not only should we pray, but also, we must.

***

"Our Father in heaven, hallowed be your name. Your kingdom come,
your will be done, on earth as it is in heaven. Give us this day our daily bread,
and forgive us our debts, as we also have forgiven our debtors.
And lead us not into temptation but deliver us from evil."

Matt. 6:9-13

Just like everything else in the spiritual life, the Bible itself gives us instruction on how to pray. In the Lord's Prayer, Jesus gives us the pattern of how we should pray. All prayer should start out with the acknowledgement that we are praying to our heavenly Father and that His name is something to be revered. *Hallowed* means to be held as sacred and honored. It seems that many people think that because God is our heavenly Father or the fact that He calls us His friend that we somehow can treat Him like He is like us. He is not. So many Christians make jokes or talk about God like He is just another buddy and casually and flippantly speak about Him like He is like us, but the fact that God has made a way for us to stand before Him blameless should in no way diminish our reverence for Him and toward Him. In fact, it should do the opposite. He didn't decrease in holiness so that we could relate to Him; God's holiness could never decrease. Instead, He created a way for us to be made holy before Him through the sacrifice of Jesus.

One very important thing to remember about prayer is this: prayer is worship, and to worship God is the reason we were created. We should worship God and honor Him with reverence and praise every time we approach Him. How could we not as we bask in the majesty of His greatness and His love for us? We should always honor our Father in Heaven with acknowledgement that the mere mention of His name is sacred. When we truly get to know the God of the Bible by reading His Word, we will see God in the proper context and understand that He not only deserves praise and honor of the highest order but that His holiness demands it.

Jesus tells us to acknowledge the sacred and holy nature of God when we approach Him and basically to give Him the proper respect that He deserves. Then Jesus tells us, as adopted children of God, that we must pray for and in light of the will of God and His kingdom purposes. When we say, "Your kingdom come, your will be done, on earth as it is in heaven" (Matt. 6:10), we are asking God to meet our needs in light of these two things. We are acknowledging that our desire to see God's kingdom come and our desire for His will to be done supersedes even our needs in life. This is why the apostles, church fathers, and many men and women through the centuries were willing to suffer and even give up their lives—because they were living to forward God's kingdom and God's will, not their own. When we pray about anything, we do it in light of these two things. Forwarding God's kingdom and His will should shape every other request we make to God, and any personal desire that undermines these two things should be abandoned in the prayer closet.

So, after we have the holy nature of God in the proper perspective and our intentions in a proper perspective as far as God's will and kingdom are concerned, then in light of this, we pray for God to supply our needs. It's interesting that in this prayer, Jesus tells us to pray for daily bread or daily provision and not anything beyond that. I believe the reason for this is found elsewhere in Scripture.

***

Two things I ask of you; deny them not to me before I die: Remove far from me falsehood and lying; give me neither poverty nor riches; feed me with the food that is needful for me, lest I be full and deny you and say, "Who is the LORD?" or lest I be poor and steal and profane the name of my God.

Prov. 30:7-9

As much as we might not want to admit it, we can quickly forget just how needy we truly are, and the place we are most likely to forget this is in abundance and blessing. God is using this life to accomplish two very important things in His children. First, God wants to have a growing and meaningful relationship with us, where we get to know the Lord more and more. He already knows us, but we will spend eternity getting to know Him. Second, He wants to conform us to the image of His Son Jesus Christ. The main point and purpose of Christian discipleship is that we are conforming to the image of Christ. If we are meeting daily with our Father in prayer, then why would we need more than daily provision? God cares about our earthly needs, but they are far less important than our spiritual needs and our spiritual eternity are to Him. The point of this life isn't to thrive in worldly, temporal things that are fading and passing away more and more every day. The point of this life is to conform to the image of Christ through His Word and through time spent with Him in our prayer closet, so we can bring glory and honor to His name and make disciples through the transforming power of the Gospel.

God sees and knows our needs before we even ask, but He is teaching us to trust in Him and to fully rely on Him. People often talk about us having a relationship with God like the nature of our relationship with Him is mutual and equal, but that is not the case. We are created beings who are needy and desperate, and we are in a relationship with a self-sufficient and eternal God Who needs nothing from us. In some ways, this relationship is very one-sided because we are the ones benefiting, learning, and growing. And as long as we understand this, we are in a good place. God's goodness is greatly displayed in the fact that while we have nothing to offer Him at all, he still bestows on us good and perfect gifts. The problem is that often what we deem as a good gift isn't what God sees as a good gift. God is perfect, and He knows what we need. But often, that is the opposite of what we want.

As we grow in the image of God, though, our wants start to become His wants, and our desires become His desires. We become less self-centered and less earthly minded, and our focus shifts from ourselves and becomes aimed at Him. The apostle Paul understood this and realized that he didn't really need anything beyond his daily provision. In his first letter to Timothy while in the middle of rebuking false teachers who were teaching that godliness is a means to financial gain, he points out the fact that we should be content with having food and clothing:

> But godliness with contentment is great gain, for we brought nothing into the world, and we cannot take anything out of the world. But if we have food and clothing, with these we will be content. But those who desire to be rich fall into temptation, into a snare, into many senseless and harmful desires that plunge people into ruin and destruction. For the love of money is a root of all kinds of evils. It is through this craving that some have wandered away from the faith and pierced themselves with many pangs (1 Tim. 6:6-10).

Pray that God would provide you with clothing, food, a place to lay your head, and your daily needs. This doesn't mean God wants you to be poor and hungry. God will provide your needs, but remember, success in this life isn't about what you have but about who you are. What I mean is that not one earthly treasure you possess will be counted toward your eternal treasure; but the conforming you do to Christ is eternal, and so is the glory you bring to His name.

Jesus then tells us to ask God for forgiveness for our debts and wrongs, ones we have made against Him and against others. When approaching God, we must always come with a heart of repentance; and honestly, when we see God for Who He is, how can we not? God is faithful to forgive those who seek His forgiveness, and we need it every day. We understand that God has forgiven us of a tremendous debt of sin, and He continues to forgive our sins daily. So, when we pray in light of this, it is a given that we would forgive others who have sinned against us in any way. No matter how wrong the sin committed against us is, God makes it clear we must forgive others. In light of a lifetime of sin which should condemn us to Hell, God forgives us, so how can we withhold forgiveness from another? Unforgiveness toward others shows that we do not truly understand or value the forgiveness God has so graciously bestowed on us. In the book of Matthew, Jesus explains this concept to us in a parable:

> Then Peter came up and said to him, "Lord, how often will my brother sin against me, and I forgive him? As many as seven times?" Jesus said to him, "I do not say to you seven times, but seventy-seven times. Therefore the kingdom of heaven may be compared to a king who wished to settle accounts with his servants. When he began to settle, one was brought to him who owed him ten thousand talents. And since he could not pay, his master ordered him to be sold, with his wife and children and all that he had, and payment to be made. So the servant fell on his knees, imploring him, 'Have patience with me, and I will pay you everything.' And out of pity for him, the master of that servant released him and forgave him the debt. But when that

same servant went out, he found one of his fellow servants who owed him a hundred denarii, and seizing him, he began to choke him, saying, 'Pay what you owe.' So his fellow servant fell down and pleaded with him, 'Have patience with me, and I will pay you.' He refused and went and put him in prison until he should pay the debt. When his fellow servants saw what had taken place, they were greatly distressed, and they went and reported to their master all that had taken place. Then his master summoned him and said to him, 'You wicked servant! I forgave you all that debt because you pleaded with me. And should not you have had mercy on your fellow servant, as I had mercy on you?' And in anger his master delivered him to the jailers, until he should pay all his debt. So also my heavenly Father will do to every one of you, if you do not forgive your brother from your heart" (Matt. 18:21-35).

In my humble opinion, the idea of withholding forgiveness from another—no matter what they have done to us or what they owe us—simply shows that we truly do not grasp the saving grace of God in the Gospel in our own lives and the degree to which we truly need it. In this parable, Jesus explains the sheer insanity by comparison of holding a sin or debt against someone else in light of our own lifetime of sin Christ has forgiven. We need God's forgiveness in our lives, and if we are truly His, we will grant forgiveness to those who sin against us as well.

Forgiving others is also a benefit to us. Holding unforgiveness produces bitterness in your heart, which will destroy you from the inside out. I am not saying in our flesh that forgiveness is always easy, especially when the wrong has inflicted great hurt and harm in your life. But if we are unable to forgive, it really just shows that we are people of this world more than people of God. There isn't a sin committed in this life that God hasn't forgiven and that God isn't willing to forgive, save one: hardening our hearts to the conviction of the Holy Spirit. It isn't that God is unwilling to forgive us but that we are unwilling to accept His forgiveness.

If you keep reading the two verses after the model prayer in Matthew 6, you will see Jesus plainly say that if we do not forgive those who sin against us, God will not forgive us.

***

"For if you forgive others their trespasses, your heavenly Father will also forgive you, but if you do not forgive others their trespasses, neither will your Father forgive your trespasses."

Matt. 6:14-15

It's very important to remember that not only does God command us to forgive, but He also empowers us to forgive. Some situations are harder to forgive than others, but there are some situations where the wrong seems unforgivable—at least by human standards. True forgiveness is a spiritual act. If we hold unforgiveness toward others, we also hold the weight of our own sin. Remember that your feelings shouldn't guide your actions. That's like saying we should let our flesh guide us in walking in the Spirit.

As we pray with God in proper perspective and in light of forwarding His kingdom and His will, we ask God to supply our needs. We prayed that God would forgive us as we forgive everyone who wrongs us, and now, we pray that God will keep us from temptation and ultimately "deliver us from evil."

***

"And lead us not into temptation, but deliver us from evil."

Matt. 6:13

The English Standard Version says, "But deliver us from evil" while the New International Version says, "But deliver us from the evil one." They mean the same thing, but one translation focuses on the one who brings evil and the other on what the evil one brings, which is evil. I like the NIV here, though, because it reminds us that we do have an adversary who wishes to destroy us, Satan. Scripture says that he is "the father of lies" (John 8:44) and that he has come "to steal and kill and destroy" (John 10:10). The devil and his demons do tempt us, but his schemes would have no power over us if we didn't have a taste for sin. In fact, although we have an adversary, the devil, and we are in a wicked and fallen world, our greatest battle of temptation lives in our own members as we battle against our flesh.

***

"No temptation has overtaken you that is not common to man.
God is faithful, and he will not let you be tempted beyond your ability,
but with the temptation he will also provide the way of escape,
that you may be able to endure it."

1 Cor. 10:13

There is no temptation in life that cannot be overcome by the surrendered life in Christ, but in the flesh, we are powerless against sin because it is part of who we are. We are born in sin. This is why Scripture says that our propensity for sin is common to mankind. We sometimes feel like our struggle is special or harder than most, but the truth is that self-denial of the sinful desires of the flesh is a losing battle for all of us unless we have supernatural help. "God is faithful . . . He will also provide the way of escape" for every situation where you are tempted. And in Christ, He has provided the ultimate and final way of escape—salvation through the cross. But this final deliverance from evil isn't the only thing to which we can look forward. God will empower us to overcome the sin in our lives, so we can bring glory to His name and forward the Gospel as He created us to do.

CONFORMING THROUGH THE SPIRIT

There are no two things more important in the life of a Christian disciple than being a dedicated student of the Scriptures and having a full and consistent prayer life when it comes to conforming to the image of Christ. But we must remember that the life that is growing in us is from the Spirit of God, and this is a mystery in so many ways.

***

"And you show that you are a letter from Christ delivered by us, written not with ink but with the Spirit of the living God, not on tablets of stone but on tablets of human hearts."

2 Cor. 3:3

It is apparent that who we are as Christians and how we grow as Christians is greatly affected and shaped by the studied, preached, and taught Word of God and by our interaction with God in prayer. But it is ultimately the internal work of the Holy Spirit in the life of the believer that does the heavy lifting. This is a supernatural process, where God Himself, through the power of His Spirit, literally works on us and in us.

Ultimately, God began a work in us, and He will finish what He started. This idea raises many questions and age-old debates that have been in Christianity for hundreds of years, but it is not my intention to focus on that here. Instead, I want to merely point out that God is the One actively transforming us and sanctifying us inside. Christianity isn't a self-development or self-betterment program. It is God actively working in the life of the believer. What's so amazing is how God uses us in this process. He uses pastors, teachers, and Christian brothers and sisters. He also uses good things as well as bad things and ultimately works them all for the good of us becoming more and more like Him.

CHAPTER 4

COME AND DIE

"I have been crucified with Christ. It is no longer I who live, but Christ who lives in me. And the life I now live in the flesh I live by faith in the Son of God, who loved me and gave himself for me."

Gal. 2:20

According to A.W. Tozer, "A whole new generation of Christians has come up believing that it is possible to 'accept' Christ without forsaking the world." Although Christianity is about having a new life in Christ, to a great degree, much of Christianity is about dying—dying to yourself, dying to sin, dying to this world, laying down your old life, and taking up a new life. The Gospel is a call to come and die, although that is not how it is represented most of the time in our culture. Often, we think about breaking free and leaving behind things we don't want in our life while we cling to the things we do want. We call this Christianity, but this is not following Jesus. Following Jesus is dying to everything you once held dear in exchange for Christ. Jesus willingly was crucified for our sins, and if we are to follow Him, we, too, must submit to a willful crucifixion, not for our sin, but to be made in the image and likeness of our Savior. Does this sound extreme to you? Well, listen to the words of Jesus Himself as He tells a crowd what following Him really requires: "'If anyone comes to me and does not hate his own father and mother and wife and children and brothers and sisters, yes, and even his own life, he cannot be my disciple. Whoever does not bear his own cross and come after me cannot be my disciple" (Luke 14:26-27).

If the only version of Christianity you have ever been exposed to is the self-centered, self-help, entertainment-driven, your-best-life-now version of Christianity, then I am sure this may come as a shock to you, but I assure you being a disciple of Jesus is an all-or-nothing proposition. Much of American Christianity is like Disneyland; it's fun, entertaining, and all about you. But to be honest, if you read the Bible and take what it says at face value, you find something much different. We see a suffering Messiah with His life aimed at a cross and a call for those who are His disciples to follow Him and do the same.

***

"And he said to all, 'If anyone would come after me, let him deny himself and take up his cross daily and follow me. For whoever would save his life will lose it, but whoever loses his life for my sake will save it.'"

Luke 9:23-24

The words of Jesus are crystal clear: if you try and hold on to this life, you will surely lose it. Some have made an art of twisting the Scripture to present a Christianity without self-denial, without sacrifice, and without the death of our flesh. But in doing so, we have also created a Christianity without passion, without power, without depth, and without beauty. To minimize the sacrificial nature of what Christ did on the cross is to minimize the beauty and power of Christianity and the very character of our Lord and Savior Jesus Christ. For us to be like Jesus, everything about our lives must be sacrificial unto His kingdom purposes. This isn't something that's above and beyond, but merely our reasonable worship to the King of glory.

***

"'All things are lawful,' but not all things are helpful. 'All things are lawful,' but not all things build up. Let no one seek his own good, but the good of his neighbor."

1 Cor. 10:23-24

We must die to everything in our life and this world—and when I say everything, I mean everything. Some things will remain dead, never to be regained, but some things will be given back to us as we learn to steward them in view of Christ. As we grow and mature in Christ through the power of the Spirit living in us, we will begin to judge all things by this measure: does this bring glory to Christ, or does it detract from His glory? Things that are sinful don't need this consideration; they should only be rejected. Some things are not necessarily sinful, but they may be something that causes you or others to stumble. Anything that mars or detracts from the glory of God in our lives should be discarded. Often when we attempt to do this and have a harder time than we expected, it is because we have stumbled on an area of our life that is rooted in a spiritual stronghold that we didn't know about. It might be a stumbling block for us that we didn't even know was there, but even if it's not, God's Word is clear; if it's a stumbling block for a brother or sister, it should be discarded as well because we are all part of the same body. According to Romans 14:13, "Therefore let us not pass judgment on one another any longer, but rather decide never to put a stumbling block or hindrance in the way of a brother" (Rom. 14:13).

The death of the flesh is a lifelong process, but it is something the Bible makes clear that we do—yes, as the Spirit sanctifies and empowers—but still, we must strive toward the mark just like the apostle Paul said that he did. Self-denial for the sake of following Jesus is a recurring theme in Scripture, and it is a direct command of Jesus. I see many Christians struggle in this area and also have been guilty myself of not denying my flesh and using the grace of God as an excuse, but this is not a proper view of grace. What makes this death we die so beautiful is what we get in exchange—Christ. We not only receive fellowship with God because of Christ, but we also receive a new life that will never pass away. In addition, we also receive immense blessing which manifests itself in us and, ultimately, through us.

Oftentimes, new Christians are told not to worry about actively denying the desires of their flesh because they are told this is a works-based theology. And sadly, this is why many Christians live in bondage to sin. All people sin, Christians and non-Christians alike, but the difference is that true converts hate sin because they love God. We sin because, frankly, we love it—or at least, our flesh does. So, what's the solution? Replace it with a greater love. Things you feed tend to grow. If you feed your flesh, your flesh will grow; if you feed your spirit, your spirit will grow. We must deny our flesh, starve it out, and let it die. But although we must deny our flesh, self-denial in and of itself isn't enough. Our focus must be less on this and more on walking in the Spirit of God. So instead of merely focusing on not doing wrong, which can be a sort of legalism, we focus on doing right out of love for God. And really, our self-denial is out of love for God as well.

Until someone sees Jesus as their all in all and realizes that what we choose in this life determines our eternity, the idea of sacrifice isn't very appealing. In fact, think about it this way: refusing to deny ourselves and obey what Jesus commands really says we don't think He is worth the sacrifice; this is idolatry. Jesus is the Treasure and Reward of the believer, and once our eyes are open to this truth, we will gladly give anything and everything to have Him. In Matthew 13, Jesus teaches a parable that explains this truth:

> "'The kingdom of heaven is like treasure hidden in a field, which a man found and covered up. Then in his joy he goes and sells all that he has and buys that field. Again, the kingdom of heaven is like a merchant in search of fine pearls, who, on finding one pearl of great value, went and sold all that he had and bought it'" (Matt. 13:44-46).

It was not begrudgingly or with reservation that the man in the parable sold everything he had to obtain the treasure; it was with joy that he did so. Once you find what you've been looking for your entire life—even if you didn't know what that was—you are filled with joy, realizing that nothing is more valuable or ever could be more valuable. Once we see Jesus as the Treasure He truly is, nothing in this world will ever compare. The reason why letting go of all of our treasures and putting our flesh to death doesn't bring us great joy is because we don't see Christ as our greatest treasure and reward. This is why we must always be careful to make sure that the person of Jesus Christ is central in all we do as Christians. If we present anything other than Christ as the center of Christianity, we are committing idolatry.

The kingdom of God isn't merely a place; it is the rule and reign of Christ Jesus Himself, which will be consummated in the second coming of Christ. He has already defeated death and brought salvation to His people in eternity; the payment for us has been made; we are simply working as we wait for the kingdom of God to come in its fullness. We are already seen as righteous in the sight of God; but when Christ returns in glory, these things that have been seen and known through a dim glass or in part will be seen by all clearly, and Christ will reign in glory and in power for eternity. This is why Christ is the Treasure of Christianity because finding Christ is finding everything. He is the Light of the world, and He is the Essence and sustaining Factor of life itself. He is Truth, and He alone is the precious Savior of mankind. This is why if we present anything other than Christ as the ultimate Reward of Christianity, we distort the Gospel and not only do damage to the purpose of salvation but also detract from its power.

The apostle Paul was at one time known as Saul of Tarsus. Saul was a devout Pharisee and had many things going for him in this life. He had dual citizenship as both a Jew and as a Roman citizen; he had social standing and affluence; he came from a respected tribe, the tribe of Benjamin. As far as the culture of his day was concerned, he had everything going for him. But he gave it all up because of an encounter he had with Jesus on the road to Damascus. Saul was a great persecutor of the Christians. He had been there when Stephen, a follower of Christ, was martyred, had been responsible for many Christians being imprisoned, and was on his way to the city of

Damascus to arrest more Christians when he had a miraculous encounter with Jesus. Because of this, everything in Saul's life changed. He had found the Treasure—or, more rightly, he had been found by the Treasure.

Jesus called him to be an apostle to the Gentiles. He became known as Paul and went from being the greatest opponent and persecutor of the church to a missionary who gave up his life of privilege and honor to preach the Gospel to the ends of the Earth. Paul went on to write the majority of the New Testament and helped start many churches in Europe and throughout the region of Asia Minor. He was beaten, tortured, imprisoned, and eventually killed because of the Gospel of Jesus Christ. And he did this willingly—joyfully even—because he saw Christ as a treasure that outshone anything and everything in this world. Matthew 13:44 has a similar ring as the words Paul speaks in Philippians 3:

> For we are the circumcision, who worship by the Spirit of God and glory in Christ Jesus and put no confidence in the flesh—though I myself have reason for confidence in the flesh also. If anyone else thinks he has reason for confidence in the flesh, I have more: circumcised on the eighth day, of the people of Israel, of the tribe of Benjamin, a Hebrew of Hebrews; as to the law, a Pharisee; as to zeal, a persecutor of the church; as to righteousness under the law, blameless. But whatever gain I had, I counted as loss for the sake of Christ. Indeed, I count everything as loss because of the surpassing worth of knowing Christ Jesus my Lord. For his sake I have suffered the loss of all things and count them as rubbish, in order that I may gain Christ and be found in him, not having a righteousness of my own that comes from the law, but that which comes through faith in Christ, the righteousness from God that depends on faith— that I may know him and the power of his resurrection, and may share his sufferings, becoming like him in his death, that by any means possible I may attain the resurrection from the dead (Phil. 3:3-11).

***

"Do not lay up for yourselves treasures on earth, where moth
and rust destroy and where thieves break in and steal, but lay up
for yourselves treasures in heaven, where neither moth nor rust
destroys and where thieves do not break in and steal. For where
your treasure is, there your heart will be also" (Matt. 6:19-21).

It is hard to follow Christ wherever He leads us when we think more
of the things He asks us to give up than we do of Him. The reason we are
willing to lay down everything to follow Jesus is because when God changes
our hearts, He also opens our eyes so we see Christ as more valuable than
anything else in this world.

Do we see Christ as everything the Word of God says He is? Creator of
the world? Sinless Sacrifice for our sin? King of all kings? The One coming to
judge the world? Our advocate in Heaven? Our only Hope for salvation and
eternal life? The other question is do we see ourselves as we truly are? Needy
and desperate for a Savior? Sinful and headed toward destruction? A creation
of God that will stand before Him one day? Also, do we see the beauty of the
Gospel? A God Who owes us nothing, Who was willing to become a sacrifice
for our sin in order that we could have eternal life and become sons and
daughters of God. Really, self-denial is simply action based on the awareness
that the Creator is so much more valuable and important than what He
created and a reciprocation of the selfless, sacrificial love He has bestowed
on us.

DEAD TO SIN

Now if we have died with Christ, we believe that we will also live
with him. We know that Christ, being raised from the dead, will
never die again; death no longer has dominion over him. For the
death he died he died to sin, once for all, but the life he lives he
lives to God. So you also must consider yourselves dead to sin and
alive to God in Christ Jesus (Rom. 6:8-11).

One reason many Christians have such a hard time counting themselves "dead to sin," as the apostle Paul says in Romans 6, is that they haven't truly died with Christ. What does this mean? Jesus considered His earthly life as a grain of wheat that was meant to die so as to reproduce itself and many times over. He was born free from sin but still endured temptation, trial, hunger, and all aspects of human life. Yes, we are born into sin, but when we are reborn into Christ, we take on a new life and a new purpose. We must realize that once we surrender to Christ, our entire life must become about dying to our old life and living in Christ and for His kingdom purposes.

If we see Christ as the Treasure He truly is and this world as the loss it is, we will find it much easier to live dead to sin. So often, though, we continue to feed our flesh and starve our spirit and then seem confused about why we are powerless to overcome the flesh. Here is a truth that we underestimate: our fallen flesh is much more sinful than we often realize. If we think of ourselves as mostly good people who, through Christ, can work at being better and better, Christ becomes just a tool we use for self-improvement. This is very far from the truth. We are actually born into sin, and that promises us ultimate death and destruction apart from the intervention of Christ. Why is it so important to understand this? Because if we think we are mostly good people who just need a little help, we devalue our need for the cross and what Christ accomplished for us through it. This is why true Christians respond with such joy and gratefulness at the Gospel because without it, we are surely lost. I'm not trying to say that working on self-improvement in one's life is wrong; I'm just saying that it has nothing to do with the Gospel—although, you wouldn't know it sitting in Sunday service in most churches today.

***

"And those who belong to Christ Jesus have crucified the flesh
with its passions and desires."

Gal. 5:24

It's interesting the words Paul uses in Galatians five when talking about the crucified flesh. He says those who belong to Christ have crucified the flesh with its passions and desires. This has much to do with our feelings—that's what passions and desires are. Before we are regenerated through Christ, these feelings are produced from our sin nature. And while it is easy to see some desires and passions are wicked, some are much more subtle. We must be on guard against things that are self-affirming and self-pleasing in nature rather than God-pleasing. I often hear professed Christians say things like, "It is God's good pleasure to give you all good things." While this statement is true if properly understood, many times, we say things like this when we are trying to promote ourselves, obtain our wants, or excuse selfish ambition. But we see in the book of Galatians that self-ambition is on par with things like sexual immorality, witchcraft, idolatry, and hatred. We will look at this in more detail in the next chapter.

***

"If we say we have no sin, we deceive ourselves, and the truth is not in us. If we confess our sins, he is faithful and just to forgive us our sins and to cleanse us from all unrighteousness. If we say we have not sinned, we make him a liar, and his word is not in us."

1 John 1:8-10

We must live dead to sin, and we must hate sin like God does. No one is sinless, but that doesn't mean we tolerate sin or live in open, ongoing sin. John the apostle makes this clear in the epistle of First John, where he talks about both of these extremes. Here, John says that we are lying if we claim that we are sinless and that His word is not in us, but in chapter three, he says if we continue sinning that we don't really know Him. Is John contradicting himself two chapters later, or is he saying something else here?

***

"No one who abides in him keeps on sinning; no one who keeps on sinning has either seen him or known him."

1 John 3:6

John is not contradicting himself. He is showing just how true the words of Jesus really are in Matthew 7:14: "For the gate is narrow and the way is hard that leads to life, and those who find it are few." The path and life of the Christian is very narrow, and our mindset must be very narrow as well. When it relates to sin, it is very true no one is sinless or ever could be. It is our awareness of this fact that leads us to repentance. Anyone who alludes to the fact or comes right out and says that they don't sin anymore is a liar. How can I say this with such authority and conviction? Because the Bible says it and the Bible is the source of all truth for the Christian life.

Many false teachers today will tell you that they are sinless. This proves one of two things: they are flat-out liars trying to build themselves up in order to sell you something, or they are self-deceived and do not have a biblical understanding of sin. Either way, they are liars. Self-deceived liars are still liars, nonetheless.

On the other hand, John is warning that continuing in an open lifestyle of sin is also damning. He says anyone who continues to sin has either seen Him or knows Him. Everything about being a Christian is so very narrow! We all sin, even once we are Christians, but the difference is that once we take on the nature of Christ, we are repulsed by it and are actively denying ourselves and putting it to death. The fact we still have sin in our members reminds us that we desperately need God and His grace every moment of our lives. And as we grow in grace, we will grow in freedom. But when we claim Christ and choose to live in an open lifestyle of unrepentant sin, we should be very concerned about the state of our soul. Once we are reborn in salvation, our love for Christ should make us hate the places where we still fall short and make us long for the day that we will be completely free from the sin we once loved.

DEATH THAT BRINGS A HARVEST

> Truly, truly, I say to you, unless a grain of wheat falls into the earth and dies, it remains alone; but if it dies, it bears much fruit. Whoever loves his life loses it, and whoever hates his life in this world will keep it for eternal life. If anyone serves me, he must follow me; and where I am, there will my servant be also. If anyone serves me, the Father will honor him (John 12:24-26).

Speaking about the purpose of His death, Jesus explains that the primary purpose of Him coming to Earth was to die. But He did not come merely to die a symbolic death, displaying His love for us—which would have been pointless and powerless—He came to die a death that would make atonement for our sins and produce a harvest of souls. The suffering and death of Jesus wasn't pointless. He was the Seed Who died to produce many other seeds, and He tells us clearly that if we are to have part in Him, we must be like Him and willingly lay down our lives in faith. He says anyone unwilling to do this will not have eternal life with Him. This life is a seed, and if we cling to it and never let it die, we will never reap a harvest and inherit eternal life. If you follow Him, you will be where He is.

In John 12, Jesus says some very staggering things by using the analogy of a kernel of wheat. In seed form, it can produce nothing without falling to the ground and dying. He explains that unless the seed dies, it will not produce a harvest. This is what Christ came to do; He died to give us life. If Christ would not have died and made atonement for our sins, we would have no chance for eternal life. We would be truly hopeless. But because of what Christ has done, we can have eternal life. However, Jesus makes something very clear; if you love and hold on to the benefits of this life, you forfeit eternal life. Jesus says we must literally hate our life in this world to have eternal life with Him. But why? It's simple: those who truly belong to Him have the Spirit of God living in them and will despise the sin and fallen nature of this world. Also, those who truly see Christ and eternal life with Him as their only treasure will realize that everything else is like a vapor and live their life accordingly. The words of Jesus are so very plain: if you love your life in this world, it is because you are not spiritually fit for eternity.

Jesus says if you love this life, you will not have eternal life. And if you really are one of His disciples, you will follow Him, live like He did, and live for what He did. Serving and following Jesus is giving up the comfort, acclaim, and respect of this world to gain approval from God. This doesn't mean we do this to earn eternal life; it means this is evidence of those who truly belong to Him. You can't build a kingdom for yourself in this life and expect to be part of His Kingdom in the next. Look at the example of Jesus and all the apostles. Jesus lived a simple life. He wasn't a rich man; He was persecuted and despised by those who were powerful in this life and who eventually killed Him. The apostles followed this example; they gave up everything to follow Jesus and preach the Gospel. They were not rich or notable; they suffered and were persecuted, and most of them were killed as well. We must live like Jesus did.

***

And by this we know that we have come to know him, if we keep his commandments. Whoever says "I know him" but does not keep his commandments is a liar, and the truth is not in him, but whoever keeps his word, in him truly the love of God is perfected. By this we may know that we are in him: whoever says he abides in him ought to walk in the same way in which he walked.

1 John 2:3-6

We must do what Jesus commands us to do in His Word and live like He did. If we want the best-case study of what this looks like in real life, we should look at the lives of the apostles. It is in dying to ourselves completely that God can use us to be part of the harvest. Many have died calling others to come and die so that they might live. In the West, we have distorted God's Word on so many levels to create a theology that lets us love our lives here and somehow still inherit eternal life; but to accomplish this, you have to call Jesus a liar.

We must live like Jesus did and obey His commandments. When you say things like this, people who love their lives and love money and the comfort of this life will say things like, "No one can live like Jesus did." And then they explain how no one is perfect and basically use this as their reason to reject this statement. But we can't reject it because it's in the Bible. John didn't say flawlessly and perfectly live like Jesus did; he said live like Jesus did. As disciples and followers of Jesus, we must model our lives after Him and follow Him. God gives us grace by His Spirit to do this, and when we fall short and repent, He forgives us. If we reject all the commandments of Jesus because we are imperfect, are we really His disciples? Nothing we do in life is done in perfection, but still, we do many things. Remember that our good works, desire, and ability to follow Jesus are not earning us salvation; they are merely evidence of it. Salvation is a gift from God. That is why if we truly belong to Him and are following Him, we will hate our life in this world because we are longing for home, which is to be where God is.

The harvest that comes from the death and resurrection of Jesus is the atonement of our sins by which we can be saved. The harvest that comes from our death is that of a life in the Spirit by which we live out the purpose of all true disciples of Jesus:

- To bring glory to God

- To conform to the image of Christ

- To make disciples and take the Gospel to the ends of the Earth.

If our life's purpose is not these three things, we are not disciples of Jesus, and our lives are ultimately meaningless to the Kingdom of God. True disciples of Jesus will strive to die to themselves, live dead to sin, and live like Jesus did as we use our lives to glorify God, become more like Him, and reap a harvest of souls, no matter what it may cost. You cannot hold on to your life and be with Christ. Jesus said that if you want to be where He is, you must follow Him.

DEAD TO LOVE FOR THE WORLD

> Do not love the world or the things in the world. If anyone loves the world, the love of the Father is not in him. For all that is in the world—the desires of the flesh and the desires of the eyes and pride of life—is not from the Father but is from the world. And the world is passing away along with its desires, but whoever does the will of God abides forever (1 John 2:15-17).

In the second chapter of John's first epistle, we see him telling us not to love the world, but if you do, it shows that God's love isn't in you. The truth is if the Spirit of God really lives in you, this world will become less and less attractive. I'm not talking about the beauty of God's creation; I'm talking about a world system that is corrupted and opposed to God Himself, even though, to some extent, the Bible says that even creation itself is corrupted by sin. Success, acceptance, influence, wealth, power, and comfort—these are the same things lost, worldly people chase after—things the Bible tells us not to follow. But many Christians do, supposedly in the name of God.

You can't pursue two different things at the same time; you can't love both God and money (Matt. 6:24); you can't hold on to your life here and have eternal life; you can't love the world or the things in the world if the love of God is truly in you.

***

"For the time is coming when people will not endure sound teaching,
but having itching ears they will accumulate for themselves
teachers to suit their own passions."

2 Tim. 4:3

The words of Jesus in the gospels are so very clear, but we so desperately want both that we fool ourselves into believing we can and then surround ourselves with teachers who validate this desire. In Christ, we must die to the love of this world. In fact, the Bible tells us to "go out from their midst" (2 Cor. 6:17) and "be holy" (1 Peter 1:16), not to camouflage ourselves and pretend we are like them. So many people within the church are desperate to be accepted by the world and the lost. It's almost like when you were in school as a kid and wanted to gain acceptance from the cool kids, but everything you did to get them to like you just makes you look more ridiculous because it was apparent that wasn't really who you were.

***

> Do not be unequally yoked with unbelievers. For what partnership has righteousness with lawlessness? Or what fellowship has light with darkness? What accord has Christ with Belial? Or what portion does a believer share with an unbeliever? What agreement has the temple of God with idols? For we are the temple of the living God; as God said, "I will make my dwelling among them and walk among them, and I will be their God, and they shall be my people. Therefore go out from their midst, and be separate from them, says the Lord, and touch no unclean thing; then I will welcome you, and I will be a father to you, and you shall be sons and daughters to me, says the Lord Almighty" (2 Cor. 6:14-18).

As Christians, we must separate ourselves from unbelievers. This doesn't mean we isolate ourselves and live in a commune somewhere; it simply means that we are separate in lifestyle and that we stand out because of it. Here is a question that all Christians should ask themselves: "What does a believer have in common with an unbeliever"? This a rhetorical question with an obvious answer—nothing! We must come out from among them and stand out. If our lives are as narrow as they should be, this will not be a problem. What does darkness have to do with light? Nothing! What does righteousness and wickedness have in common? Nothing! We are only lying to ourselves if we believe anything different.

We must come out from among the world and die to self and sin and live our lives conspicuously for Christ. Christianity is about our new life in Christ, but it's also about putting an old life and nature to death. Letting go of yourself and this world for Christ is the most beautiful and fulfilling thing you will ever do, and it's also a clear and direct command of our Lord Jesus. Giving up this life for salvation and eternal life in Christ is the greatest exchange that you will ever make. God is saying we do this to have communion with Him. If we separate ourselves from this world, He "will walk among [us] and will be [our] God, and [we] shall be [His] people" (Lev. 26:12). If we want to be sons and daughters of almighty God, we must "touch no unclean thing" and come out from among the world (2 Cor. 6:17).

CHAPTER 5

WALKING BY THE SPIRIT

But I say, walk by the Spirit, and you will not gratify the desires of the flesh.
For the desires of the flesh are against the Spirit, and the desires of the Spirit
are against the flesh, for these are opposed to each other, to keep you from
doing the things you want to do. But if you are led by the Spirit,
you are not under the law.

Gal. 5:16-18

The apostle Paul makes a grand declaration in the beginning of the fifth chapter of Galatians. He exclaims that it is for freedom that Christ has set us free. But free from what? The curse of sin that comes from our inability to fulfill the law of God. Christ didn't abolish the Law; He perfectly fulfilled it. The only man who could ever live up to the Law was the Lawgiver Himself, the God-man Jesus Christ.

***

"Do not think that I have come to abolish the Law or the Prophets;
I have not come to abolish them but to fulfill them."

Matt. 5:17

Jesus Christ gave us this freedom from sin by fulfilling the Law, which made Him uniquely qualified to be the atoning sacrifice for our sin. To break the curse of sin and death, Jesus Himself became a curse. If we understand the holiness and worthiness of the sovereign God of the universe, the idea of this should shock us. He Who knew no sin from all eternity became sin for us. He carried the guilt and shame of all humanity past, present, and future. Christ did on the cross what we couldn't do for ourselves.

***

"Christ redeemed us from the curse of the law by becoming a curse for us—for it is written, 'Cursed is everyone who is hanged on a tree'—so that in Christ Jesus the blessing of Abraham might come to the Gentiles, so that we might receive the promised Spirit through faith."

Gal. 3:13-14

So, Christ redeemed us and saved us from the curse of the Law and the penalty of death for our sin to include the Gentiles, which simply means non-Jews, in the blessing of Abraham. This blessing is that God would set apart a people for Himself and that He would be with us. But ultimately, God will live in us and transform us. This group of people that Christ will save unto Himself will be made up of Jews and Gentiles alike, people from every nation and tribe of the world. By faith in Christ, we receive the promised Spirit, which takes up residence in us and sanctifies us. Salvation is an unearned gift of God given to us through His grace; it is a gift from God afforded to us by the work of Christ on the cross. Sanctification is also a gift from God that is a work done by Christ through the Spirit. That is why the Scripture says in Hebrews 12 that Jesus Christ Himself is the Author and Finisher of our faith:

> Therefore, since we are surrounded by so great a cloud of witnesses, let us also lay aside every weight, and sin which clings so closely, and let us run with endurance the race that is set before us, looking to Jesus, the founder and perfecter of our faith, who for the joy that was set before him endured the cross, despising the shame, and is seated at the right hand of the throne of God (Heb. 12:1-2).

Christ set us apart to be His people, His inheritance; this is what freedom in the Spirit is—freedom from sin and freedom from death to be raised to a new life in Christ. We have two natures in us: the corrupt sin nature we were born with and the Spirit of God we received once we were reborn and regenerated through Him. It's very important to look at this as a supernatural rebirth—something that was dead being raised to life—because our human nature will inevitably be drawn toward believing our works earned us something.

This is part of the curse of our sin nature. We believe in our goodness because we often compare ourselves to others rather than to God and His standard, which is perfection. We want our works to validate us when we feel we are doing well or at least better than others, but we want grace when we realize we fall short. But the truth is we always fall short. If we see ourselves as we truly are, unable to do good in God's sight, we will understand that we could never come close to righteous on our own through works. Remember what the Scripture says: "We have all become like one who is unclean, and all our righteous deeds are like a polluted garment. We all fade like a leaf, and our iniquities, like the wind, take us away" (Isa. 64:6).

Paul spends much of the letter to the Galatians explaining that if you think living a good life can earn you salvation, you don't understand the Gospel and are not truly saved. Thinking we can earn salvation is the opposite of saving faith. We are wholly and fully saved by grace through faith in Christ Jesus. And although He is saying good deeds and a moral lifestyle cannot save us, he isn't saying it's okay to live the opposite of that. Saying that good works can't save you doesn't mean we live an immoral lifestyle. Salvation and sanctification are supernatural gifts.

Paul is saying that in our fallen state, we don't want to be good and can't be good because it's not in our nature. We are sinful by nature, so doing good doesn't save us. That's not to say that we can't do any good deeds in our fallen state. People who are not Christians do good deeds all the time. Doing good and truly being good by God's standard are two different things. God's standard is moral perfection in action and intention. Any good we do is still tainted with corruption and sin.

We are actually given a new nature in salvation and are regenerated or reborn. Our new nature has new affections and desires. So, good works don't save us; they are evidence that we are saved. In a very real way, we are called to starve our old nature and feed our new nature. If we walk by the Spirit, the Scripture says we will not gratify the desires of the flesh. But the flesh is still waging war against the Spirit; they are contrary to each other.

Under inspiration of the Holy Spirit, Paul says if you try to earn your salvation by your own merit, you are judged by the Law; but if you are led by the Spirit, you are not under the curse of the Law. Why? By faith, your trust is in the One Who became a curse for us. Jesus set us free from this curse. This doesn't mean the Law is bad; the Law is the perfect character and decree of a holy God. It's a curse to us because we are unable to live up to it. The fate of those who ignore the Law is the same of those who think they can live up to it—judgment and condemnation. It's only through Christ we are saved, and it's only by His Spirit we are sanctified.

SLAVES TO RIGHTEOUSNESS

> What then? Are we to sin because we are not under law but under grace? By no means! Do you not know that if you present yourselves to anyone as obedient slaves, you are slaves of the one whom you obey, either of sin, which leads to death, or of obedience, which leads to righteousness? But thanks be to God, that you who were once slaves of sin have become obedient from the heart to the standard of teaching to which you were committed, and, having been set free from sin, have become slaves of righteousness (Rom. 6:15-18).

As fallen humans, our idea of freedom is answering to no one and being able to do what we want, but really, this is a false dichotomy. There are only two options: slavery to sin or slavery to righteousness. Righteousness literally means "right standing with God." So, either we are right with God, or we are not. All of mankind has sin; we are born into it, and because we are fallen and corrupt, we continue to sin. We can't help it because it is our nature; so, in a very real way, we are slaves to sin.

Here is an analogy that explains what I mean. When we are born, we are born into sin; we are slaves to sin, and it is unavoidable. This is like being outside in a violent and heavy rainstorm, and you are in an open field with nothing around for miles and miles except for one building. There is literally nothing you can do to avoid getting wet. You can lay down, stand up, run in circles, close your eyes; but no matter what you do, as long as you are outside, you will continue getting wet. The only way to stop getting rained on is to go inside the building. In the same way, we are either slaves to sin or slaves to righteousness; you are either outside the building getting wet or inside the building drying off. There isn't another option.

In the Gospel, we are pardoned from our sin because of what Christ did on the cross, so we are free from the penalty of our past sin. But we have also been regenerated and given a new nature by which we are not only free from the penalty of past sin and future sin, which is death, but we are also free from the sin nature with which we were born. It doesn't mean we are incapable of sinning; it merely means that now we have the capability to live a righteous life, and as we are sanctified through the Spirit in Christ, we will eventually bear more and more fruit. Walking by the Spirit is about bearing fruit and, over time, being transformed into the image of Christ, our Teacher and Master. Although the strength and life-sustaining power of a tree is in its root system, the ultimate evidence of what kind of tree it is appears in its fruit.

***

But the fruit of the Spirit is love, joy, peace, patience, kindness, goodness, faithfulness, gentleness, self-control; against such things there is no law. And those who belong to Christ Jesus have crucified the flesh with its passions and desires. If we live by the Spirit, let us also keep in step with the Spirit.

Gal. 5:22-25

Walking by the Spirit is living the life God has intended for us to live. When we look at the fruit of the Spirit as unregenerate people, we think we understand it. Words like *love, joy,* and *kindness* are familiar to us, but our understanding of these concepts and character traits are as corrupt as the sin nature with which we are born. Before Christ, we think we know what love is and what joy and peace are. But there really is no way to fully understand these things in a real way, much less experience them disconnected from their source, Who is God Himself. It's like trying to describe the beauty of a sunset when you have been blind your entire life. You can describe it based on what you have been told, but your description will always lack because you haven't ever really experienced it for yourself.

We might think we know what the love of God is based on what our fallen and human mind perceives, but until we are in Christ and of the Spirit, we could never really know that God defines what love is because He is love. The fruit of the Spirit is the evidence of our salvation that manifests itself in our lives. We bear the fruit of God because we are connected to God. It's not acting like something or doing something; it's becoming something and being something. It all begins with the love of God that we perceive and receive in the Gospel. As we see God as holy and just, we fear the Lord; and we fear Him all the more as we see ourselves in light of this. Our lives are not holy or good. Our sinful lives are deserving of condemnation and punishment from God. This is why when we truly see the grace of God in light of these things, we get a glimpse of the magnitude of God's love for us. We have done nothing but offend God, but the Scripture says, "But God shows his love for us in that while we were still sinners, Christ died for us" (Rom. 5:8).

Through this sacrificial and amazing love, Christ atoned for our sin and gave us a new heart. Regeneration literally changes us. To harden your heart to the Gospel is to harden your heart to the love of God. The fruit of the Spirit is the very character of God toward us, and once we are born again, it becomes our new nature and character. This new nature is born in us—not all at once, but in a real way. The love we receive from God in the Gospel transforms us and changes us. Because of this love, we are filled with joy, true joy—a joy that is supernatural. It's something the world cannot give to you and something the world could never take away. For the first time, you know peace, real peace, a peace the Bible says is beyond human comprehension or understanding—a peace that understands that no matter what happens in this life, we have the reward of eternal life with Christ. Because of this, we can be assured, even in hardship and trial.

So, because we have been transformed by the love of God, we should be filled with love, joy, and peace. And because of this, in turn, we will be patient, kind, good, faithful, gentle, and, ultimately, self-controlled. These are the attributes of God, and if God really lives in us, we should be displaying this fruit in an ever-increasing way. The fruit of the Spirit mentioned in Galatians 5 aren't good deeds Christians should try to do as much as they are the fruit or evidence of who you really are. If the Spirit of God lives in you, it will manifest itself in this way.

So, why do we still sin? Because although the Spirit of God is in us, we are still in our fallen and corrupted flesh. This is why Paul tells us that if we walk by the Spirit, feed the Spirit, and build up the Spirit, we won't gratify the desires of the flesh. This has to do with the freedom that comes from obeying God and being a slave to righteousness. Why does this not seem to be the case for so many Christians? Often, we foolishly believe we can walk by the Spirit as we continue to gratify the desires of our flesh, but we can't be fully devoted slaves to two opposing things; you are a slave of the one you obey.

Galatians 5:24 says, "And those who belong to Christ Jesus have crucified the flesh with its passions and desires." God gives us the power and desire to do this, but this is a place where we are being told to do something. We are being told to crucify our flesh with all of its passions and desires. God does the work of salvation and regeneration, and in response, He tells us to crucify our own flesh and deny ourselves. That encompasses so much, but according to Jesus, this appeared to be a prerequisite to following Him: "Then Jesus told his disciples, 'If anyone would come after me, let him deny himself and take up his cross and follow me. For whoever would save his life will lose it, but whoever loses his life for my sake will find it" (Matt. 16:24-25).

Walking in the Spirit is about walking in the love of God and living a life of love and obedience toward God. The idea of self-denial of the flesh only sounds unappealing if you are still living for yourself. If you love God and have been reborn in Christ, you will desire to please Him and grow in sanctification. As Christians, we must live a life of self-denial and obedience toward God. This is what it means to love God instead of merely saying empty words: "'Whoever has my commandments and keeps them, he it is who loves me. And he who loves me will be loved by my Father, and I will love him and manifest myself to him" (John 14:21).

The idea of self-denial for the sake of love isn't foreign to our human understanding of love; in fact, it is the center of it. Parents deny themselves of things to provide for their children; husbands and wives deny themselves of other intimate relationships when they commit to be married for life. We view sacrifice in relationships as romantic and admirable. So how much more sense does that make in our relationship with the sovereign and holy God of the universe, Who saved us and changed us and sacrificed greatly on our behalf.

Sometimes, we use the word *relationship* much too broadly when we talk about God. We do have a relationship with God, but we must realize that we can't think about our relationship with God like we think of our human relationships. God is not like us. Our relationship, fellowship, and worship of God is not on our terms but on His. It's not a relationship between peers or equals. It's not a friendship based on mutual respect. God is above us, and we are below Him in every way. But although we have nothing of value to give Him, He still wants to fellowship with us. We will look into this thought deeper in the next chapter.

WALKING IN LOVE

"Therefore, be imitators of God, as beloved children. And walk in love, as Christ loved us and gave himself up for us, a fragrant offering and sacrifice to God."

Eph. 5:1-2

Love is the central and overarching principle of Christianity, so we must be mindful of it in all other things we do. Since love is such an important part of walking in the Spirit, we must be very careful to define it biblically and correctly right from the start. Often, people wrongly define love from a worldly point of view, instead of a biblical point of view, and then we determine what is right and wrong, good and bad from this flawed perspective. We must understand everything from the perspective of Scripture. The Scripture is God's holy and inspired Word and should define the reality of a Christian's life in every way.

Instead of trying to determine anything from our flawed and corrupt mind, we must let the Scriptures renew and transform our mind, but walking in the Spirit of God starts with a transformed or regenerate heart. We cannot perceive love or truth in a real way before this because in a very real way, we are dead. So, once we have the Spirit of God living in us, we can perceive the truth of God's Word. Many Christians fall in the trap of letting unregenerate people define love for them and then spend their life trying to fit God into that box. How, then, do we define love? It's simple; we look to the Scripture.

***

Beloved, let us love one another, for love is from God, and whoever loves has been born of God and knows God. Anyone who does not love does not know God, because God is love. In this the love of God was made manifest among us, that God sent his only Son into the world, so that we might live through him. In this is love, not that we have loved God but that he loved us and sent his Son to be the propitiation for our sins.

1 John 4:7-10

God is Love! God is perfect, and so the perfect definition of love is God Himself. And 1 John 4 shows us that the most excellent example of this for us to examine is that of Jesus Christ coming and atoning for our sins on the cross. So, we can't judge if God is loving based on our fallen, human perception of love; but instead, we determine what love is based on our understanding of God. The love of God for us is inseparable from the Gospel; it's through the lens of what Jesus did for us on the cross that we should view all this. When we realize that all humanity deserves punishment and judgement because of our sin, our perspective about God changes. When we look at ourselves as good and innocent, we think of life as being unfair in so many ways; but when we see the reality that we are the creation of God, who have rebelled and wronged Him and who actually deserve wrath and judgement, we see how good and loving God really is.

So, we love God because He loved us first, and from this principle, the Christian life is oriented. Our love for others is born in God's love for us. Walking in the Spirit is Christ fulling the law through us. What do I mean by this? When Jesus was asked what the greatest commandment was, He replied, "'You shall love the Lord your God with all your heart and with all your soul and with all your mind. This is the great and first commandment. And a second is like it: You shall love your neighbor as yourself. On these two commandments depend all the Law and the Prophets'" (Matt. 22:37-40).

Jesus basically summed up the Ten Commandments in light of the overarching principle of love. If you look at the two tables of the Ten Commandments in the Exodus 20, it is divided in this way: commandments about our relationship with God and commandments about our relationships with people. The first four commandments are in regard to how we should relate to God, and the last six are how we are to relate to people.

COMMANDMENTS ON HOW WE RELATE TO GOD:

1. "You shall have no other gods before Me" (v. 3)

2. "You shall not make for yourself a carved image" (v. 4)

3. "You shall not take the name of the LORD your God in vain" (v. 7)

4. "Remember the Sabbath day, to keep it holy" (v. 8)

COMMANDMENTS ON HOW WE RELATE TO PEOPLE:

1. "Honor your father and your mother" (v. 12)

2. "You shall not commit murder" (v. 13)

3. "You shall not commit adultery" (v. 14)

4. "You shall not steal" (v. 15)

5. "You shall not bear false witness against your neighbor" (v. 16)

6. "You shall not covet" (v. 17)

If we biblically understand God and if we biblically understand love, we will see that if we love the Lord with everything we have—heart, soul, and mind—we fulfill the first four and most important commands of the Ten Commandments. And from that, we will be able to love our neighbor as ourselves (Mark 12:31) or the way God has loved us, by which we fulfill the last six commands of the Ten Commandments. This brings up the question, can we really love that way?

I often hear people say we don't have to keep the Ten Commandments; we just have to love God and love people, but they are obviously using a flawed and human definition of love. Jesus is requiring something of us that is humanly impossible. He is pointing us back to the Law, which exposes that we are unable to keep it and shows our need for something or someone outside of ourselves to save us. He points us to the Law and Prophets, which point us to Him.

No person has ever loved the Lord God "with all of your heart and with all of your soul and with all of your mind" (Matt. 22:37) perfectly and at all times. Jesus was the only One Who ever did that. That is what it means to fulfill the Law of God. The Gospel was always God's plan to save, sanctify, and perfect a people for Himself. Walking in the Spirit of God is all about being grafted into the life of Jesus, the death of Jesus, and the resurrection of Jesus; and this is merely evidenced in our love and obedience to God and how we love and treat others. Remember, God is Love. If we are connected to this love, we have life.

***

"I am the true vine, and my Father is the vinedresser. Every branch in me that does not bear fruit he takes away, and every branch that does bear fruit he prunes, that it may bear more fruit. Already you are clean because of the word that I have spoken to you. Abide in me, and I in you. As the branch cannot bear fruit by itself, unless it abides in the vine, neither can you, unless you abide in me."

John 15:1-4

If we are grafted into the Living Vine—as Jesus refers to Himself in John 15—we are progressively being sanctified, bearing the fruit of Christ through the Spirit and being pruned of parts and branches that are not bearing fruit and have no evidence of life.

If we are truly saved, it means we are connected to the Source of life, and we will bear fruit that is in kind with that. No branch can bear fruit on its own; it must remain in the vine. If we are connected to the Source of life, we will bear fruit. The evidence of our salvation in Christ is His Spirit living in us. Walking in the Spirit means bearing the fruit of the Spirit; this is the evidence that you are truly connected to the Source of life, the Living Vine, Jesus Christ.

Walking in the Spirit means you have evidence that you really are connected to the Life source. You can look at a plant and pretty easily tell if it's connected to life or not by its color, its leaves (or lack thereof), and if it is visibly connected to anything or not. The evidence, or the fruit, of a life that has the Spirit of God living inside of it is really no different.

Galatians 5:22-25 shows us how loving God and loving others is the ultimate evidence of the Spirit living within us. It's through the love God displayed for us in the Gospel that we are reborn and come to life, and the evidence of this love in your life is the first and most important indication of whether the Spirit of God lives within you or not. Those who have responded to the love of God will love God and love others. The Bible says we show God we love Him through worship and obedience to His Word, and we love others by loving them as we love ourselves.

Love is the overarching evidence of a life connected to the Vine, a life walking according to the Spirit. A life that has surrendered to the love of God in the Gospel is a life that for the first time knows joy, real joy—not happiness that can be waned by circumstance, but a supernatural joy that nothing in this world could ever give you and nothing in this world could ever take away. This perfect love that comes from God and produces joy also gives us perfect peace. People who know God's love know a peace that passes all human understanding. A lost and rebellious heart that has found peace with God cannot be shaken. If you don't have peace in your heart, it's because you still value something above God because to be at peace with God is more valuable than anything else.

God loved us first. Because we have received His love, we love God and the world at large. Because of this transformative love, we are filled with joy, and we are finally at peace with God. If we are transformed by His love for us in the Gospel, filled with the joy of our salvation, and know that our soul is at peace with God, we will naturally be patient, kind, good, faithful, gentle, and self-controlled. The fruit of the Spirit are not character traits that help us become good Christian people; it's merely evidence that we have truly been transformed by God, that His Spirit lives in us, and that we are truly connected to Jesus, the Source of life.

As long as we are in our earthly bodies, we will be at war with sin; but if we walk according to the Spirit, the Spirit that has set us free, we will gratify the desires of the flesh less and less. Through prayer and fellowship with God and the study and obedience of His Word, God prunes us. He cuts away the parts of our life that are brittle and dead, which invigorates the good parts with new life. As we crucify the flesh and dead parts are cut off, we will bear more and more fruit, just like a tree that is pruned. As long as we stay connected to the Vine, we will bear fruit in this life; and one day, when we shed this earthy body, we will be completely free of sin forevermore.

CHAPTER 6
WORSHIP AND FELLOWSHIP

"'But the hour is coming, and is now here, when the true worshipers will worship
the Father in spirit and truth, for the Father is seeking such people to worship him.
God is spirit, and those who worship him must worship in spirit and truth.'"

John 4:23-24

You will often hear people today say things in regard to God like, "It's about relationship, not religion." I believe I understand what they are trying to say to some degree, but it is very important that we understand the meanings of words and flesh out the intentions of what we are saying, so we can have full understanding. I would say that true Christian discipleship is about both. The term *religion* simply means a system of beliefs that you adhere to and live by, and this is true about Christianity. The distinction is that we don't earn salvation by doing these things; we do these things out of obedience to God because we love Him and because He is worthy. There is also an indication that if we have no desire to obey God, we are probably not really Christians.

"Religion says: I obey therefore I am accepted. Gospel says: I am accepted
therefore I obey."—Timothy Keller

Often people try to use the Pharisees as the example of why religion is bad and relationship is good, but the Pharisees, to a great degree, were corrupt and used their position to keep people from a relationship with God rather than using their position to draw people to God. They were teaching salvation by works and through keeping the Law. But this doesn't mean we discard religion altogether. We reject false, hypocritical religion but not true religion as outlined by the Scripture. Christ didn't come to abolish the Law but to fulfill it.

Christianity is about having a relationship with God, but God Himself dictates the terms of that relationship. To understand how to have a right relationship with God, we need to understand a set of beliefs, which is the Christian religion. The Bible tells us how we are to have a relationship with God, that God expects obedience from us, and that there is a prescribed way He wants to be worshiped. The Bible tells us Who God is, what He expects from those who belong to Him, and how He commands us to worship Him.

The problem with the word *relationship* is that we can be tempted to think about God like one of us, as though we are equals in this relationship or that this relationship is the same as relationships we have with others. This is not the case. God is holy, sovereign, and worthy of all worship and praise. He is perfect, and we are not; His love is perfect, and ours is not. He is not like us, so we shouldn't view this relationship like any others we have. We must fear and reverence the Lord and honor Him as God. This is why our relationship with God starts with worship, and this is why we must see our worship and how we relate to God through the Gospel. We must see God as holy, sovereign, and perfect and see ourselves in light of God. We are sinful, wicked, and undeserving of anything except for judgment and condemnation. And in light of these two things, we see God's grace. Christ came and died to save us, not based on anything we have done or ever will do, but simply because He loves us. This is the reservoir from which our worship and adoration for God must come.

In our relationship with God, everything must begin with our worship of God, and we must make sure our acts of worship are biblical. If we think that we can live any way we want and worship however we please, we are wrong. Worship isn't just confined to what we do when we meet together for church, although that is an important part of it. Worship is living our lives in honor of and in obedience to God. We worship God not just because of what He has done—although, we do that as well—but also, primarily, because of Who He is. God is holy, and God is worthy. He deserves all praise and adoration simply because He is God.

Oftentimes, people focus their worship on how God has blessed them and the good things in their life. While it is important to be thankful and grateful for the blessings we receive in this life, it's important to remember that God is worthy of praise if He blesses us or if He doesn't, when life is good and when life is hard. He is worthy either way. This is also an important part of faith because God's goodness transcends our circumstances. This is what kept Job throughout his trial. He understood the sovereignty of God, but he also trusted in the goodness of God, not based on his circumstances but based on Who God is. In Job 13:15, we read, "Though he slay me, I will hope in him: yet I will argue my ways to his face" (Job 13:15).

Worship isn't a gift we give God; it's something we owe Him. Worshiping God is based on knowing Who God is; if you really know Who God is, you will fear Him, worship Him, and trust Him because He is good. Usually, when people talk about worship, they are referring to corporate worship, but this is just a small part of it. In a very real way, worship is about pouring our life out in honor of the one Who poured His life out for us. We deny ourselves and our flesh, and we live our lives unto God. Paul tells us in Romans 12:1, "I appeal to you therefore, brothers, by the mercies of God, to present your bodies as a living sacrifice, holy and acceptable to God, which is your spiritual worship." Basically, he says self-denial and living in obedience to God is just basic Christianity.

Often, people who don't really see God for Who He is have a hard time with this because they view God as Someone Who is here to serve them and is here to help them, instead of Someone we were created to worship and serve. So, when things don't go the way they want, they often become disillusioned with God. I will probably say this several more times before this book is done, but all true worship and all good theology begins and ends with a proper view of God. Our view of God has a great impact on how we worship Him, how we view the world, and how we live. If we have a low view of God, this is usually exposed by how we worship and view His Word. People who have a low view of God's Word are typically people who also engage in worship that pleases them rather than being bothered with whether it is pleasing to God. These sorts of people think that anything that pleases them must please God because God loves us. This is a very self-centered way to look at life, and this is the epitome of being self-righteous. The self-righteous person assumes God is on their side; the righteous person is concerned with making sure that they are on God's side.

TRUE AND PROPER WORSHIP

"O God, you are my God; earnestly I seek you; my soul thirsts for you;
my flesh faints for you, as in a dry and weary land where there is no water."

Psalm 63:1

We use the term *relationship* a lot in Christianity, but I prefer the term *fellowship*. You have a relationship with everyone you know. Some are good; some are bad. The devil has a relationship with God; it's not a good one, but he has one. I'm not trying to say it's wrong to use that terminology. I just feel like in discussion about God and the worship of Him, the word *fellowship* is better. Fellowship implies a presence, and it's personal.

In Christian discipleship, the true Christian is reborn into Christ; and in this rebirth, we gain new appetites and desires, one of which is an unquenchable longing for God and a right standing with God. To some degree, every person ever created longs for God. We long to know the purpose of life; we long to know where we belong in this life; we long for meaning; and we long for satisfaction. And to a degree, we long to know God. But what separates a regenerate person from a non-regenerate person is this: the regenerate person longs to be right with God and to be at peace with God, while a non-regenerate person does not have the same desire.

***

"'Blessed are those who hunger and thirst for righteousness,
for they shall be satisfied.'"

Matt. 5:6

Those who long and desire to be at peace with God will be filled. This is the power of the worship of and fellowship with Almighty God. Gospel-centered worship is always focused on the greatness of God, our need for Him, the love of God, and the grace of God. Worship is all about God, not about us. We will look deeper into the concept of hungering and thirsting for righteousness in the next chapter of this book.

***

For you, O Lord, are my hope, my trust, O Lord, from my youth. Upon you I
have leaned from before my birth; you are he who took me from my mother's
womb. My praise is continually of you. I have been as a portent to many, but
you are my strong refuge. My mouth is filled with your praise, and with your
glory all the day.

Psalm 71:5-8

We see our need for God in salvation from our sins but also in all things from our birth. We need God for the air we breathe, the gravity we use, the planet on which we were born, the sight for our eyes. Every detail of our existence depends on the sovereignty and power of God. Having a high and proper view of Who God is also reveals to us that we are not owed anything from God. Everything down to the blessing of even being created is a mercy and blessing from God, and any gift beyond that is an unearned blessing that testifies to His goodness.

***

"'But the hour is coming, and is now here, when the true worshipers will worship the Father in spirit and truth, for the Father is seeking such people to worship him. God is spirit, and those who worship him must worship in spirit and truth.'"

John 4:23-24

What does it mean to worship God "in spirit and in truth"? This Scripture in John 4 is part of the story of Jesus' encounter with a Samaritan woman at a well at the edge of town. As Jesus talks with this woman, they discuss the difference between the way the Samaritans worship God and how the Jews worship God. She is basically arguing with Jesus about which is the right way to worship, but she is talking about ceremony and location, while Jesus is talking about something deeper and much more real—matters of the heart.

To worship in spirit means that we worship God from our heart and with sincerity; it isn't just ordinances, traditions, and rituals. There is nothing wrong with church liturgy and formality as long as they are observed with passion and sincerity toward God. True worship must originate from our love for God, reverence for His holiness, acknowledgement of His goodness, and place of lowliness before Him. To worship God in spirit, we must have fellowship with Him and know Him, and the more we know Him, the more we will love Him and be grateful for our salvation. But to worship Him in spirit and from the heart, we must know Him in truth. This where a lot of people get off-base.

We should be passionate and zealous in our worship of the Lord, but we must make sure we are worshiping Him in truth and according to Who He really is. The Holy Spirit reveals to us the beauty and value of God—a beauty and value we cannot see before we are in Christ. If we are worshiping God and our idea of God is not biblical, we are committing the gravest of sins. Biblical truth should be the basis of all we believe and all we do as Christians. The Bible is God's direct revelation given to us through the Holy Spirit which reveals to us the one and true God. Our worship of God does cause emotion and even excitement at times, but if that emotion and excitement arises from thoughts that are not biblically sound, we are not worshiping God; we are worshiping an idol.

The idea that because our emotions are sincere, our worship is pleasing to God is simply wrong. People are sincerely wrong about things all the time. That is why our fellowship with God and our worship of God must be grounded in sound doctrinal and biblical truth; otherwise, we are not really worshiping the triune God; we are worshiping an idol of our own construction. Here is where it gets easy to err. We often use Christian lingo when naming our idols. From our vantage point, we can clearly see that the Israelites were wrong to worship the golden calf that was constructed while Moses was on the mountain receiving the Law of God (Exod. 32). But when we take a closer look at the story, we realize that it really isn't far away from some modern viewpoints and methodologies on worship.

Moses had gone up on the mountaintop to meet with God to receive the Ten Commandments, and while he was up there, the Israelites got tired of waiting on Moses to come back. So to appease the people, Moses' brother, Aaron, found a practical means. He told them to take off their golden earrings and jewelry to melt down and construct a golden calf for the people to worship. And guess what they called it? Yahweh, which is translated "Lord" in our English Bible. And the people declared, "These are your gods, O Israel, who brought you up out of the land of Egypt" (Exod. 32:4). They made something of their own creation and called it the Lord and even attributed God's mighty works to it as validation.

Any time we worship God in a way that is unpleasing to Him or in a way that is in contrast to His Law or His Word, we blaspheme His name. So often, we construct idols in modern worship and in our lives and attribute them to the Lord, but anything that contradicts His sacred Scripture and His holy nature isn't from God but from the evil one. The fact that something feels good or right to you doesn't make it right. People will often try and explain away unbiblical worship and unbiblical lifestyles by saying that God has confirmed it in their spirit, but what they are really saying is that it feels good to them. Here is a good point to remember: your feelings are not the Holy

Spirit! This is so very common today—people being led by their feelings and calling it the Holy Spirit. This is very dangerous and is the ultimate human deception—to believe that something is right because they feel like it is right or to give the idol of their feelings the name God and be led by it. This is the most common form of Christian idolatry today.

The Word of Truth, the Scripture, was authored by the Spirit of truth, the Holy Spirit, so these things will always be in agreement and often will be in opposition of your feelings and your flesh. Oftentimes, Christians will feel like they have somehow matured past the need for biblical guidance in these areas, but this is absurd. To "worship God in spirit and in truth," we must sincerely worship God from our heart according to His Word.

HE IS ABOVE, AND WE ARE BELOW

"Yours, O Lord, is the greatness and the power and the glory and the victory
and the majesty, for all that is in the heavens and in the earth is yours. Yours
is the kingdom, O Lord, and you are exalted as head above all."

1 Chron. 29:11

One of the most concerning trends in some modern churches is the lack of reverence and awe for the God we serve. Some believe that since we are being adopted into the family of God as sons and daughters, we shouldn't view ourselves as servants of the Lord. This posture, in my opinion, greatly affects the way we worship. It is a view that elevates man's place and lowers God's. Although there are a few Scriptures that mention that we are no longer slaves and that God considers us sons, daughters, and friends, this doesn't mean that we are equal with God or anywhere close. We are new creatures in Christ, and one day, we will be forever free from sin, which is amazing. But we will always be created beings. Having too high of a view of ourselves makes worship more of a love relationship between equals rather than us humbly, graciously, and gratefully worshiping God as King.

Sometimes, this elevation of ourselves is subtle, but it is damaging and dangerous and has a negative effect on our view of God and how we worship Him. If our worship is Gospel-centered, we will see God as He is: the Creator of the universe, self-contained, self-sustaining, timeless, perfect, holy, worthy, sovereign. And we will see ourselves as we truly are: desperate, needy, sinful, lost, completely dependent on the goodness and grace of God, weak, fragile. So then, seeing God as He truly is and seeing ourselves in light of that, we see His grace and love toward us as an amazing gift, and from this comes true and genuine worship—worship filled with reverence, gratefulness, and awe.

This is what Christ-centered worship looks like. Our worship is centered around Jesus. This is the problem with the attractional, purpose-driven, seeker-sensitive church; it is fueled by creating an experience that is enjoyable for the churchgoer rather than focusing on a worship that honors and pleases God.

***

"For great is the LORD, and greatly to be praised; he is to be feared above all gods."

Psalm 96:4

When our corporate worship service is centered around the feelings and experiences of the lost people we hope to attract to our church instead of on the God we are supposedly worshiping, in a very real way, we are worshiping them and not God. For this reason, I don't really care for the terminology of calling our church services a worship experience as so many do today. It sounds like an attraction at Disneyland rather than the corporate gathering of the saints to worship God.

Biblical worship should be Christ-centered and man-denying. It should lift the name of Jesus high and be focused on Him. It should be doctrinally sound and theologically rich. It should be unifying to the body and not aimed at bringing us into unity with the world. Often when talking about worship, we are referring to music, but music is only a part of the corporate worship of God. Although I think there are wrong ways to worship as far as corporate worship goes, I am not saying there is only one right way. Throughout the world, the body of Christ is very diverse and is infused with many different generations, races, and cultures; this makes the body of Christ beautiful and full, but this also can create many challenges. Although churches have many different styles and structures, I believe that it is okay and to be expected. As long as worship is reverent, biblical, Gospel-focused, and Christ-centered, I believe it is acceptable to God.

THE STUDY OF THEOLOGY IS WORSHIP

The term *theology* is widely misunderstood. It is greatly misused today in our modern church culture. I often hear it used in very negative ways, like it is some outdated system or tradition, but the term *theology* simply means "the study of God." Knowing God should be the highest aim of our life, so the study of God is very important. To "worship God in spirit and in truth" requires us to know God, and this requires being a devoted student of God's Word. If you think it doesn't matter what we believe about God or that there isn't a right and wrong way to worship Him, you are sadly mistaken. What we believe about God determines, in a very real way, where we will spend eternity. God is not like us; He is far above us and chose to make Himself known in a few ways, but the primary way is through His Word. Many people today use the term *theology* as if it were a dirty word or somehow at odds with our relationship and worship of God, but we must remember that the richness of our relationship and the height of our worship is determined by the depth of our theology.

When we worship God in a way that is pleasing to us and view God in a way that we like, we are not worshiping God; we are really worshiping ourselves. We must study to show ourselves approved (2 Tim. 2:15), and if we really want to know Who God is and what pleases Him, the study of theology will be one of the great joys of our lives. You can't properly worship Someone you don't know. The better you know God, the deeper and richer your worship of Him will be.

CHAPTER 7

THE EVIDENCE OF A GOSPEL-TRANSFORMED LIFE

"Blessed are the poor in spirit, for theirs is the kingdom of heaven. Blessed are those who mourn, for they shall be comforted. Blessed are the meek, for they shall inherit the earth. Blessed are those who hunger and thirst for righteousness, for they shall be satisfied. Blessed are the merciful, for they shall receive mercy. Blessed are the pure in heart, for they shall see God. Blessed are the peacemakers, for they shall be called sons of God. Blessed are those who are persecuted for righteousness' sake, for theirs is the kingdom of heaven. Blessed are you when others revile you and persecute you and utter all kinds of evil against you falsely on my account. Rejoice and be glad, for your reward is great in heaven, for so they persecuted the prophets who were before you."

Matt. 5:3-12

Matthew 5-7 contains the longest recorded sermon Jesus ever delivered. It is referred to as the Sermon on the Mount because of the place where He delivered it. These three chapters of Scripture are in a very real way the manifesto of Jesus that highlights the Gospel, the kingdom of God, and Christian living.

In the first part of chapter five, Jesus outlines certain character traits that seem to have staggering eternal consequences. How many times as a young Christian did I just brush past these power words Jesus spoke? I think oftentimes, we think we come into Christianity knowing what the Gospel is and what it means to be saved, and our eyes are not really open to developing this out. But honestly, when Jesus Himself makes statements about eternity, we should probably pay very close attention.

Matthew 5:1-12 is referred to as the Beatitudes, and the meaning is pretty easily surmised by how it sounds. These are the attitudes, or the posture, of the Christian life. This is really a character sketch of what a Gospel-centered life really will look like. Verses three and ten both end with the phrase "for theirs is the kingdom of heaven," so in a very real way, Jesus is saying this is the way to Heaven. This is how Jesus starts His three-chapter Gospel presentation by saying that this is how the life of a true Christian will look and then concludes this sermon in chapter seven by saying:

> "Everyone then who hears these words of mine and does them will be like a wise man who built his house on the rock. And the rain fell, and the floods came, and the winds blew and beat on that house, but it did not fall, because it had been founded on the rock. And everyone who hears these words of mine and does not do them will be like a foolish man who built his house on the sand. And the rain fell, and the floods came, and the winds blew and beat against that house, and it fell, and great was the fall of it" (Matt. 7:24-27).

So, hearing these words and putting them into practice is essential for salvation and to inherit the kingdom of Heaven. We need to pay close attention to make sure we understand what this portion of Scripture truly means because the stakes are very high. Jesus proclaims Himself as the Substance of the Gospel, where He presents Himself as the Way and says that His words are the imperative and exclusive way to life.

THE BEATITUDES

"Blessed are the poor in spirit, for theirs is the kingdom of heaven."

Matt. 5:3

Right from the beginning, we see that much of what Jesus says is countercultural and is in complete opposition to conventional and worldly wisdom. The very first thing we must realize in order to inherit the kingdom of Heaven is that we are spiritually bankrupt. We bring nothing to the table. We must see ourselves as needy and desperate. I mentioned this in previous chapters, but having the right view of God makes us realize how much we need Him. We are hopeless without Him in every possible way, and the beginning of the Christian is us seeing our need.

God doesn't need us for anything. Knowing this should be very humbling to us. Without fully realizing this, we will never see grace for the gift it truly is. Undeserved, unearned, and beautiful.

***

Thus says the LORD: "Heaven is my throne, and the earth is my footstool; what is the house that you would build for me, and what is the place of my rest? All these things my hand has made, and so all these things came to be, declares the LORD. But this is the one to whom I will look: he who is humble and contrite in spirit and trembles at my word.

Isa. 66:1-2

What have we ever done for God that really benefited Him? The answer to the question is nothing. This is the lens by which we should view God because once we realize God owes us nothing, we begin to see how truly good to us He is. So, who is it that God will look upon with His favor? Those who are humble and contrite in spirit and who tremble at His Word. In other words, those who are "poor in spirit." It is only those who realize they are lost without God and that they are not good enough to earn righteousness. Anyone who believes that their goodness is good enough will not enter the kingdom of Heaven.

***

"Blessed are those who mourn, for they shall be comforted."

Matt. 5:4

Throughout the Old Testament, when the Israelites fell into sin, they were told by God through the prophets to mourn and lament their sins. In Matthew 5:4, Jesus gives a powerful admonition: "'Blessed are those who mourn, for they shall be comforted.'" They will be justified before God; this is what it means to repent of our sin. Jesus expands on this idea in a parable He told in Luke 18:

> He also told this parable to some who trusted in themselves that they were righteous, and treated others with contempt: "Two men went up into the temple to pray, one a Pharisee and the other a tax collector. The Pharisee, standing by himself, prayed thus: 'God, I thank you that I am not like other men, extortioners, unjust, adulterers, or even like this tax collector. I fast twice a week; I give tithes of all that I get.' But the tax collector, standing far off, would not even lift up his eyes to heaven, but beat his breast, saying, 'God, be merciful to me, a sinner!' I tell you, this man went down to his house justified, rather than the other. For everyone who exalts himself will be humbled, but the one who humbles himself will be exalted" (Luke 18:9-14).

The Pharisee wasn't poor in spirit, nor was he repentant over his sin. People who think that they are good at heart are deceived because instead of comparing themselves to God's standard, they compare themselves to others. We mourn because through the power of the Gospel, we see our inability to be holy. Matthew 5:4 is often quoted to say that God will comfort us when a loved one dies or when some other tragedy befalls us. And while this is not necessarily wrong, it is superficial because at its core, all death and tragedy is caused by sin. To truly be comforted is to once and for all be free of the bondage of sin and death. As Christians, our hope and faith are tied up in the fact that when Christ returns for us, that promise will become a reality.

Now in a very real way, everyone mourns in some regard because of sin. You cannot go through this life without tragedy or loss of some kind. But the difference between the righteous and the unrighteous is that everyone mourns because of the effects of sin, but the righteous person mourns over sin itself. Those who repent and truly mourn because of their sin—the sin that separates them from God—will be comforted.

***

But he gives more grace. Therefore it says, "God opposes the proud but gives grace to the humble." Submit yourselves therefore to God. Resist the devil, and he will flee from you. Draw near to God, and he will draw near to you. Cleanse your hands, you sinners, and purify your hearts, you double-minded. Be wretched and mourn and weep. Let your laughter be turned to mourning and your joy to gloom. Humble yourselves before the Lord, and he will exalt you.

James 4:6-10

The only comfort God has for the sinner is the Gospel. We spend so much time trying to convince unregenerate people to live holy lives, or we often try and comfort sinners in their sin. But the truth is the Gospel is the only hope there is for the lost. We must truly repent of our sins; and in repentance, we find refreshing comfort and security of our salvation. Jesus died to forgive our sins once and for all, and it is by this act, we are justified before God. His death and resurrection bring us comfort knowing that our sins will not be held against us on the day of judgment.

***

"Repent therefore, and turn back, that your sins may be blotted out, that times of refreshing may come from the presence of the Lord, and that he may send the Christ appointed for you, Jesus, whom heaven must receive until the time for restoring all the things about which God spoke by the mouth of his holy prophets long ago. Moses said, 'The Lord God will raise up for you a prophet like me from your brothers. You shall listen to him in whatever he tells you. And it shall be that every soul who does not listen to that prophet shall be destroyed from the people.'"

Acts 3:19-23

Jesus came to seek and save sinners. So, the idea that we can present the Gospel without talking about sin is foolish. It is because of sin that we needed a Savior in the first place. One of the main differences between those who are lost and those who are saved is that those who are saved mourn and lament over their sin because they truly love God and know that sin is what separates us from Him.

***

"Blessed are the meek, for they shall inherit the earth."

Matt. 5:5

The idea that the meek will inherit the Earth is completely at odds with the conventional wisdom of the world. Throughout the history of the world, people have fought to take hold of and to hang onto power. In our world, we admire the strong, powerful, and prosperous. It's survival of the fittest. Do leaders rise to power in our world by being meek? Do Wall Street traders and corporate CEO's rise to the top of industry by being meek? When you look through human eyes at this world, does it seem like the meek are inheriting the Earth? The answer is no. That is why this statement by Jesus is so staggering. Often, you hear people murmuring about the fact that it seems that the wicked are prosperous while the righteous suffer in this life. I guess the question is are you living for this life or for the reward and promise of the life to come?

Jesus wants us to remember that we are not living for this life and our reward is not in this world. To be meek in this life, you must trust God. Trust that He is in control. Trust that He will keep His promises to us in the next life. We must take Him at His Word. This is what true faith looks like. If we are living only for this life, we had better get all we can out of it while we can; but if we are living for eternity and truly believe God's Word, we will trust Him, and this will produce a posture of meekness.

***

Be still before the Lord and wait patiently for him; fret not yourself over the one who prospers in his way, over the man who carries out evil devices!

Refrain from anger, and forsake wrath! Fret not yourself; it tends only to evil.
For the evildoers shall be cut off, but those who wait for the Lord shall inherit
the land. In just a little while, the wicked will be no more; though you look
carefully at his place, he will not be there. But the meek shall inherit the land
and delight themselves in abundant peace.

Psalm 37:7-11

The more you know and trust God, the easier it will be to be humble and meek. Seeking power and security in this life shows that you don't really trust God, and it also shows that you don't realize that everything in the world belongs to God. Every created thing, including us, belongs to God. In the end, God will distribute judgment and blessing according to His Word and His will, so if Jesus says "the meek shall inherit the earth," then they will. God will do as He sees fit because He is God. We are meek because we trust Him, and our meekness is evidence that our life is centered around our faith in God. It also bears witness to the fact that we are following in the footsteps of our Savior, Jesus Christ.

***

The earth is the Lord's and the fullness thereof, the world and those who dwell
therein, for he has founded it upon the seas and established it upon the rivers.
Who shall ascend the hill of the Lord? And who shall stand in his holy place?
He who has clean hands and a pure heart, who does not lift up his soul to
what is false and does not swear deceitfully. He will receive blessing from the
Lord and righteousness from the God of his salvation. Such is the generation
of those who seek him, who seek the face of the God of Jacob. Selah.

Psalm 24:1-6

We also have a great living Example of this—our Savior, Jesus Christ. In meekness, He became lowly and took on flesh like one of the beings He created. He lived a life of meekness, restraining His power for the sake of those whom He came to save. He endured suffering, hunger, pain, and scorn because He had nothing to prove, just a mission to accomplish. He was beaten, accused, and killed and never raised a hand or even His voice because He was living to fulfill the will of His Father in Heaven. We, too, have a mission and a purpose in this life, and it is the mission and purpose of every Christian in the world—to bring glory to God, to conform to the image of Christ, and to make disciples. If we are living for this and not ourselves, we will produce the fruit of meekness because we are living for God and others and not ourselves.

Remember this meekness isn't something you do to earn salvation; it is evidence of your trust in God and in His Word. This is why the meek person doesn't need to assert themselves or promote themselves. Meekness isn't given to selfish ambition and doesn't put too much value in this life and this world because the truly meek person isn't living for this life but is looking toward a city whose Builder and Maker is God Himself.

***

"Blessed are those who hunger and thirst for righteousness,
for they shall be satisfied."

Matt. 5:6

The greatest evidence of a truly regenerate person is that they will want to be righteous. So, what does it mean to be righteous? Righteousness means to be in right standing with God or to be justified before God. Apart from the Gospel of Jesus Christ, this is impossible. If we could be right before God without the Gospel, then Jesus wouldn't have had to come and die. All things outside of Christ are subject to judgment and condemnation, but because of Jesus, we are justified before God the Father.

Here is such a great promise from God. Those who really long to be right with God will be because of Christ. We can take great comfort in the fact that God will never turn away anyone who longs to be right with Him. God will not turn away from anyone who has a repentant and contrite heart who confesses Christ as King. Here is the problem, though: most don't want this.

In a very real way, on some level, everyone longs for God, even if they don't know that's what they are longing for.

Don't confuse what I'm saying. I do not mean that people are actually seeking God. There are no seekers. But everyone longs for and chases things only God can provide. We all want peace, joy, love purpose, etc., but we don't want what they are attached to—God. Every human has recognition that they are missing something in this life, and we try to fill that hole with many different things. Some try to fill it with relationships and sex. Some try to fill it with the pursuit of success, career, and accomplishments. Some try to feel it with noble social causes that make them feel good about themselves. Some try to fill it with their children or hobbies. Some will try to fill it with shopping, eating, drinking, or abusing drugs; but nothing will ever satisfy. Not that all these things I listed are bad or wrong, but none of them could ever fill you up and give you eternal satisfaction.

The reason it doesn't say those who hunger and thirst for *God* but instead says *righteousness* is that to some degree, everyone longs for God or at least what He can provide, but those who will be filled are those who long to be right with God and to be at peace with God.

There are also those who, to some degree, believe in and acknowledge God. They hope to fill themselves by doing good deeds and participating in religious activity. If there is a Hell to escape, they also want to be saved from that. Over the years, I have had many discussions with many people who believe you can be saved without following Jesus or that their good deeds or their parents' good deeds have some bearing on where they will spend eternity. Jesus is the only Way to the Father, and you must know God and be known by Him to be saved from your sin. The sad reality is you can't call Him Savior if you don't call Him Lord. Matthew 7:21-23 warns:

> "Not everyone who says to me, 'Lord, Lord,' will enter the kingdom
> of heaven, but the one who does the will of my Father who is in
> heaven. On that day many will say to me, 'Lord, Lord, did we not

prophesy in your name, and cast out demons in your name, and do many mighty works in your name?' And then will I declare to them, 'I never knew you; depart from me, you workers of lawlessness.'"

We are saved by grace, through faith, in Christ but the life that has truly been redeemed by Christ will desire to be right with God and will live a life of obedience. We will love the Law of the Lord and strive to live a life that pleases Him because we love God as well. This is the difference between true righteousness and self-righteousness. Self-righteousness says, "God is on my side." True righteousness says, "I will be careful to make sure I am on God's side."

One of the greatest joys of our Christian life is knowing that because of our salvation through the substitutionary atonement of Jesus Christ, we are justified before God, and nothing in this life will be able to snatch us from His hand.

***

"Blessed are the merciful, for they shall receive mercy."

Matt. 5:7

At this point, we can begin to look at the rest of the Beatitudes in light of being filled with righteousness. We could say those who are filled with Christ's righteous will be merciful, or those who are filled with Christ's righteousness will be pure in heart, or those who are filled with Christ's righteousness will be peacemakers, or those who are filled with Christ's righteousness will be persecuted. Like the fruit of the Spirit we read about in Galatians 5, this is evidence of someone who has been regenerated, justified, and is in the process of being sanctified.

We can also say this another way; these are attributes of Christ that now reside in us. Mercy is one of the main components in our relationship with God and one of the most powerful, undeserved gifts He has given to us. God's mercy is evidence of His goodness in our lives. When we show mercy, it is also evidence of God's goodness because how could we refuse anyone mercy when we ourselves have been shown so much mercy by God? Mercy is evidence that we have Christ living in us, and a lack of mercy may indicate the opposite is true. I qualify this statement by saying that it *may* indicate this because we are being sanctified and are still growing. But if mercy is not part of your character to others, you should examine your heart. Jesus gives us a parable in Matthew 18 that explains the effect God's mercy should have on our life:

> Then Peter came up and said to him, "Lord, how often will my brother sin against me, and I forgive him? As many as seven times?" Jesus said to him, "I do not say to you seven times, but seventy-seven times.
>
> "Therefore the kingdom of heaven may be compared to a king who wished to settle accounts with his servants. When he began to settle, one was brought to him who owed him ten thousand talents. And since he could not pay, his master ordered him to be sold, with his wife and children and all that he had, and payment to be made. So the servant fell on his knees, imploring him, 'Have patience with me, and I will pay you everything.' And out of pity for him, the master of that servant released him and forgave him the debt. But when that same servant went out, he found one of his fellow servants who owed him a hundred denarii, and seizing him, he began to choke him, saying, 'Pay what you owe.' So his fellow servant fell down and pleaded with him, 'Have patience with me, and I will pay you.' He refused and went and put him in prison until he should pay the debt. When his fellow servants saw what had taken place, they were greatly distressed, and they went and reported to their master all that had taken place. Then his master summoned him and said to him, 'You wicked servant! I forgave you all that debt because you pleaded with me. And should not you have had mercy on your fellow servant, as I had mercy on you?' And in anger his master delivered him to the jailers, until he should pay all his debt. So also my heavenly Father will do to every one of you, if you do not forgive your brother from your heart" (Matt. 18:21-35).

Remember that we must view this parable, as well as the Beatitudes, through the lens of the Gospel. How could someone forgiven of such a great debt be so hard-hearted toward someone who owed them such a small debt? The answer is that they couldn't without taking for granted the mercy that the king had shown him. And the same goes for us. If we are unable to be merciful and forgiving to those who have wronged us in this life, it shows that we take for granted the great debt we have been forgiven and the value of the sacrifice it took to forgive those sins. Jesus is saying that a heart that is unwilling to forgive shows they don't see the value of their own forgiveness, which is a good indication that they are not truly saved. A little later in the Sermon on the Mount in Matthew 6, Jesus plainly says an unmerciful and unforgiving heart will not be forgiven: "For if you forgive others their trespasses, your heavenly Father will also forgive you, but if you do not forgive others their trespasses, neither will your Father forgive your trespasses" (Matt. 6:14-15).

Those who are truly saved have the heart of Christ and will forgive because Christ is forgiving. Those who have the heart of Christ will show mercy because Christ is merciful. To be saved from the penalty of your sins, you must first see them and repent of them. If you are not willing to extend that grace to someone else, it shows that your heart hasn't been changed by the love and grace of God. The mercy we extend to others is an overflow of the mercy we have been extended by God in the Gospel.

***

"Blessed are the pure in heart, for they shall see God."

Matt. 5:8

This verse should make the honest person very uncomfortable. It doesn't, though, because most people in our world have an unbiblical view of their own heart. Most people feel deep down that they are mostly good, although the Bible says something entirely different. We are so full of self-esteem, positive affirmation, and self-love psychology that the idea that our heart is not pure is very troubling to think about for most of us. To truly follow Christ, we must acknowledge Him as our Authority, and we must realize that our hearts are wicked and our minds corrupt. This is what necessitates the Gospel.

**

"The heart is deceitful above all things, and desperately sick:
who can understand it?"

Jer. 17:9

"[Our] heart is deceitful . . . and desperately sick." That prognosis sounds very grim to me, and it should because it is. Even as Christians, our heart can sometimes convince us that right is wrong and wrong is right. We need God's Word to light our path, to tell us what is right and what is wrong, and to conform us to the image of Christ. Our hearts and feelings will lie to us, but God's Word, as illuminated by the Holy Spirit, shows us the truth of reality.

All through the Sermon on the Mount, Jesus is directing us to focus on the heart and not the exterior. The exterior merely bears fruit according to what's at the root. One of the most important parts of presenting the Gospel is knowing how greatly and desperately we truly need it. It is through the conviction of sin that the Spirit makes us aware of the true condition of our hearts. This is why Jesus says things like, "Everyone who looks at a woman with lustful intent has already committed adultery with her in his heart" (Matt. 5:28), or if you are so angry with your brother, you curse him in your heart and have committed murder (Matt. 5:21-23). Who is pure in heart? No one except the God-man Jesus Christ. Who has seen God? No one except Jesus.

This was one of the reasons that Jesus was so harsh with the scribes and Pharisees. They made so much effort to live blameless lives in front of others but had no interest in changing their hearts. They were so blinded by pride that they didn't recognize the very God they had supposedly dedicated their lives to serving. Matthew 23:25-26 says, "'Woe to you, scribes and Pharisees, hypocrites! For you clean the outside of the cup and the plate, but inside they are full of greed and self-indulgence. You blind Pharisee! First clean the inside of the cup and the plate, that the outside also may be clean'" (Matt. 23:25-26).

The heart is the part of who you are in the most secret place of your life, the thoughts no one else will ever see—your true feelings and your true mind, not your polite exterior. It is the part of you known only to you and God; but unlike you, God has an objective and perfect view, whereas you do not. If we are honest, this fact alone will humble us and keep us permanently dependent on God.

Pure means perfectly undefiled. So, although we feel like we are pretty good, when we compare ourselves to the purity and perfection of God, we see we are not. Purity means perfection in substance, not how we feel about ourselves. We are not pure in heart because we are contaminated by sin, and this is why we are separated from God. This is also the mechanism by which we see our need for God. If only the pure in heart will see God, then this means that no one will see God, unless God Himself intervenes on our behalf. And He did through the cross.

***

"No one has ever seen God; the only God, who is at the Father's side,
he has made him known."

John 1:18

God is pure in heart and perfect in every way; this is why He is the only Way. God sent His Son to live a pure and perfect life and then to take the penalty for mankind, so we could see God. What an amazing Gospel promise that we will be able to see God because of Jesus. No one has seen God but the Son, but through fellowship with the Son, we will see God.

***

"Jesus said to him, 'I am the way, and the truth, and the life.
No one comes to the Father except through me.'"

John 14:6

The only way we will see God is through Christ. There is no other way. Many people subtly reject the Gospel for this reason; they believe that they are pure in heart apart from Christ's atoning work on the cross, and this a quiet and polite way of rejecting their need for Him. Remember that Jesus looks at the deepest recesses of the heart and judges us based on His standard, which is complete perfection and undefiled purity. Remember that this is Jesus' Gospel presentation to us. A good Gospel presentation should always show how needy we are and how hopeless we are without Jesus and should point us toward Him.

***

"Beloved, we are God's children now, and what we will be has not yet appeared; but we know that when he appears we shall be like him, because we shall see him as he is."

1 John 3:2

Here is the good news: those who are reborn into Christ can come to God based on His purity instead of their own; and because of this, they will see God. Through the Gospel of Jesus Christ, not only does God forgive our sins and give us a new heart, but He also does it for the purpose of making us His children.

***

"'Blessed are the peacemakers, for they shall be called sons of God.'"

Matt. 5:9

As children of God, we should be like Christ and have character attributes resembling His. Jesus brought peace to the world, a peace that reconciles individuals to God, and as His children, we should be peacemakers in this sense as well.

***

"And, as shoes for your feet, having put on the readiness given by the gospel of peace."

Eph. 6:15

We should have our feet fitted with the "gospel of peace," which reconciles men to God. However, this does not mean that God came to bring world peace or that we should seek peace at any cost. We cannot compromise truth for the sake of peace. The peace we bring is the Gospel. I have heard progressive and unbiblical churches use Scriptures like Matthew 5:9 out of context to try and argue that we should tolerate wickedness for the sake of peace and unity or that we should not argue about doctrine because we are supposed to be peacemakers, but this is simply not true. In fact, Jesus Himself made this very clear as He quotes from the book of Micah:

> "Do not think that I have come to bring peace to the earth. I have not come to bring peace, but a sword. For I have come to set a man against his father, and a daughter against her mother, and a daughter-in-law against her mother-in-law. And a person›s enemies will be those of his own household. Whoever loves father or mother more than me is not worthy of me, and whoever loves son or daughter more than me is not worthy of me. And whoever does not take his cross and follow me is not worthy of me. Whoever finds his life will lose it, and whoever loses his life for my sake will find it" (Matt. 10:34-39).

This doesn't mean we should be intentionally hostile to people; in fact, the opposite is true. We are to be peace-loving, kind, and humble at heart. We should be bold and fearless when it comes to standing for the truth of God's Word and preaching the Gospel. In every other place, we should be kind, meek, and humble. Remember that the fruit of the Spirit of God living in you is love, joy, peace, patience, kindness, goodness, gentleness, faithfulness, and self-control. So, longing to be at peace with people in your life is important, just not at the expense of the truth, which is the only thing that can make them reconciled with God. It's through the Gospel alone that people find peace with God. This message is very hostile to most people, so very often, it will cause offense instead of peace. That is why as Christians, we must remove every other obstacle so that nothing in our life interrupts or interferes with the message of the Gospel.

***

"For in him all the fullness of God was pleased to dwell, and through him to reconcile to himself all things, whether on earth or in heaven, making peace by the blood of his cross."

Col. 1:19-20

God is a God of peace. This is why He sent His Son to die for us and to reconcile us to Himself, so that He might have friendship and fellowship with us. Now, we are His ambassadors of reconciliation, calling people to be reconciled with God. We are to live like Christ did and live holy lives that don't detract from the Gospel we preach. Our hearts must be obviously different from the world, and Jesus gives a few examples of what the life of true sons and daughters of God will look like as we deal with people inside and outside the faith.

***

"You have heard that it was said, 'An eye for an eye and a tooth for a tooth.' But I say to you, Do not resist the one who is evil. But if anyone slaps you on the right cheek, turn to him the other also. And if anyone would sue you and take your tunic, let him have your cloak as well. And if anyone forces you to go one mile, go with him two miles. Give to the one who begs from you, and do not refuse the one who would borrow from you. You have heard that it was said, 'You shall love your neighbor and hate your enemy.' But I say to you, Love your enemies and pray for those who persecute you, so that you may be sons of your Father who is in heaven. For he makes his sun rise on the evil and on the good, and sends rain on the just and on the unjust.

Matt. 5:38-45

When I was young in the faith, I used to think that the words of Jesus here were so extreme, but that was because I still had my focus on this life instead of the life to come. When we take to heart Jesus' words to lose our lives in exchange for eternal life in Christ, we realize that the concept of loving our enemies is also evidence that we have died to the love of this world and are living for the next life. We weren't saved by justice, and we haven't received what we deserve—eternal punishment. We were saved by grace through forgiveness we didn't earn or deserve. So, in a very real way, we are willing to endure suffering for the truth to draw people to the truth because we are living to be like Christ. We love our enemies because we know that at one time, we were enemies to God as well, and it was only by God's grace that we were saved.

*****

"Blessed are those who are persecuted for righteousness' sake,
for theirs is the kingdom of heaven."

Matt. 5:10

Through the last several verses, we have seen what a Gospel-centered life will look like. Also, we see the staggering gravity of what is attached to each of these statements as they end with remarks like, "for theirs is the kingdom of heaven" and "they will be called children of God." To inherit the kingdom of Heaven, you must realize that you are spiritually bankrupt, and that apart from Christ, you could never be saved. You must mourn over your sins and repent, and only then will you find eternal comfort.

You must be meek, trusting in Christ alone for your salvation, realizing that those who trust Him will inherit the Earth—not the strongest or the smartest but, instead, those who are meek because they trust the Lord. Jesus tells us that those who truly long to be righteous before God will be filled. And those who are right with God will be merciful because of the mercy they have been shown. Also, they will be able to see God because of the new heart of purity they have because of Christ. They will be people who long to see people find the same peace with God that they have found.

Finally, we come to the final evidence of someone who is right with God, who stands for the truth of God's Word, and who fearlessly lives out and proclaims the Gospel—persecution. The Beatitudes start and end with this promise: "for they will inherit the kingdom of heaven." But to inherit the kingdom of Heaven, you must truly rely on Christ for your salvation and your righteousness before God. It is impossible to live in a fallen, sin-filled world proclaiming the truth of the Gospel and standing uncompromised for God's Word and not endure some persecution. In the second epistle Paul wrote to Timothy, his son in the faith, he said, "Indeed, all who desire to live a godly life in Christ Jesus will be persecuted" (2 Tim. 3:12).

As a true follower of Jesus, you can expect persecution from two places— from pagans, who deny God, and from false religion, which distorts God. Being persecuted because of standing for and declaring the truth of God's Word is no new thing. The job of the prophets of the Old Testament was to proclaim God's Word, and more often than not, they were not well-received for the same reason the truth of God's Word isn't received today—because we love ourselves, our sin, and our idols. Jesus says that those who long to be right with God will be filled and that those who are filled should expect persecution.

The first three Beatitudes expose the awareness a person who has responded to the Gospel has about the state of their soul apart from Christ. John Piper calls this a state of holy emptiness. The Gospel exposes our hunger and need for God, and the fourth Beatitude promises that those who hunger to be right with God will be filled.

The next three Beatitudes are not about the emptiness that brings us to God but about the fullness we have because we are filled with the righteousness of Christ. So, the question is, if the result of your surrendered life in Christ is mercy, purity, and peace, why would anyone persecute you? It's really very simple: it's the root of where it comes from that causes offense. It's the exclusive nature of Jesus and the narrowness of His Gospel. People aren't offended by the fruit of your life as much as they are by the implications that fruit has on their lives. If Jesus really is the only way to fill the emptiness inside them, then it has eternal implications for them. And even if they deny it deep down, they know it. So, they are offended by you because you are merciful and forgiving, because you are at peace, and because you are pure in heart. But really, it is because you are fulfilled by the Master you serve, the same Master they reject.

True Christians are striving to live lives that please their Master and King; this is what makes us stick out, and this is also one of the things that bring conviction to those who are outside of Christ. We are salt and light. By contrast, our saltiness shows the tastelessness of others. The truth and light of our lives shine light into the dark places in the lives of others. A set-apart life of holiness and obedience to God shows what's lacking in the lives of those outside of Christ, a neediness and lack they do not want exposed; so, they hate us and persecute us, just like they did Jesus and the prophets that came before Him.

***

"Blessed are you when others revile you and persecute you and utter all kinds of evil against you falsely on my account. Rejoice and be glad, for your reward is great in heaven, for so they persecuted the prophets who were before you."

Matt. 5:11-12

This isn't saying that anyone who is persecuted will be blessed. People are persecuted all the time for reasons that have nothing to do with the Gospel of Jesus Christ. What it is saying, though, is that if you are persecuted because you live for Jesus and live like Jesus, you will be blessed and will inherit the kingdom of Heaven. In a very real way, persecution is a great indication you are truly living for God. But the reverse is also true if you live in a world full of sinners and your lifestyle doesn't stand out and your words don't bring offense to anyone ever. You are probably not living a set-apart life and aren't fulfilling the Great Commission.

In America, we have invented a gospel that is not offensive to anyone and that doesn't require a life of holiness, discipleship, self-denial, or following Jesus. It is a gospel you can preach and have all men speak well of you. This is a false gospel, forged in the pits of Hell, and for those who follow it, that's exactly where it leads. Jesus says you will be blessed when people insult you, persecute you, and say all kinds of evil against you because of Him. In fact, we should rejoice because our reward in Heaven will be great. It doesn't say anything about being blessed because people think well of you or speak well of you. So if this is true, why is this our aim so often in the American church? Maybe it's because we truly believe that we can serve two masters.

***

"'No one can serve two masters, for either he will hate the one and love the other, or he will be devoted to the one and despise the other. You cannot serve God and money.'"

Matt. 6:24

All through the Beatitudes, Jesus is showing us that it is impossible to be saved without Him and that it is impossible to be saved without being changed. Salvation through Jesus Christ is about getting a new heart. If we still look, feel, and act just like the unbelievers do, Jesus is saying we haven't been changed by the Gospel. This lesson is teaching us that being saved is much more than merely saying you believe in Jesus or reciting a salvation prayer—a prayer that is not even in the Bible.

***

"Not everyone who says to me, 'Lord, Lord,' will enter the kingdom of heaven, but the one who does the will of my Father who is in heaven. On that day many will say to me, 'Lord, Lord, did we not prophesy in your name, and cast out demons in your name, and do many mighty works in your name?'

And then will I declare to them, 'I never knew you;
depart from me, you workers of lawlessness.'"

Matt. 7:21-23

At the end of the Sermon on the Mount, Jesus says many will call Him Lord but will still not inherit the kingdom of heaven. In the Beatitudes, Jesus shows the evidence of what a truly converted life will look like. It's not a road map of actions to becoming saved but a list of evidence of what a truly regenerated person will look like. But it can also serve to bring conviction to those who misunderstand what a Gospel-transformed life is and draw them to repentance. All though the Sermon on the Mount, Jesus points to Himself and to His words as the only way to life.

***

"Everyone then who hears these words of mine and does them will be like a
wise man who built his house on the rock. And the rain fell, and the floods
came, and the winds blew and beat on that house, but it did not fall, because
it had been founded on the rock. And everyone who hears these words of
mine and does not do them will be like a foolish man who built his house on
the sand. And the rain fell, and the floods came, and the winds blew and beat
against that house, and it fell, and great was the fall of it."

Matt. 7:24-27

He ends the Sermon on the Mount by saying that anyone who hears these teachings and puts them into practice is like a wise man who built a house on a rock-solid foundation. No matter what storms come, his house will stand. But anyone who does not put these teachings into practice is like a man who builds his house on the sand. When the storms come, his house will come down with a great crash.

The evidence of a Gospel-transformed life is laid out for us in the Beatitudes, all through the Sermon on the Mount, and, really, in the entire New Testament. There is no regeneration without transformation, and if we have been saved through day-by-day sanctification, we are being changed to become like our Savior. If you haven't done a thorough inspection of the foundation of your life to make sure it looks like Jesus says it should, stop building, tear down everything you have already built, and start over. If the foundation is wrong, the house will not stand the test of time.

We are talking about eternity, so what you are building on is everything. Jesus must be the Foundation on which we are building, and nothing is more important than this. It doesn't matter how good the building supplies are and how well you build them; if the foundation isn't secure and strong, it is all for nothing. Does your life bear the evidence of a good and strong foundation? If Jesus truly is the Foundation of your life, your life will look like the description Jesus gives in Matthew 5:3-10. If it doesn't, pray and repent because eternity hangs in the balance.

CHAPTER 8

HOLINESS

*"Do not be unequally yoked with unbelievers. For what partnership has
righteousness with lawlessness? Or what fellowship has light with darkness?
What accord has Christ with Belial? Or what portion does a believer share
with an unbeliever?"*

2 Cor. 6:14-15

Before we can talk about personal holiness in the life of the believer, we
must start with the holiness of God. There is no way to overstate the fact that
God is not like us. He is the standard for everything, and He is perfect in every
way. He is above all things, over all things, and outside all things. The triune
God—Father, Son and Holy Spirit—have always been and will always be. God
has many attributes. He is Love; He is good; He is eternal; He is sovereign;
He is immutable; He is incomprehensible; He is omniscient (all-knowing),
omnipresent (everywhere at once), and omnipotent (all-powerful). There are
many more attributes that make up God Almighty, some that we can reflect in
our lives to a small degree because we are made in His image but others that are
far beyond us because He is God and we are mere created beings.

Although all of God's attributes are equally important to defining His
character, no single attribute of God is focused on more in the Scripture or
is more crucial to our understanding and worship of Him than His holiness.
The holiness of God is the reason for the cross. I truly believe most people

have trouble with the necessity of the crucifixion because they don't see the value of God and His moral perfection.

To be holy means to be distinct, set apart, and in a class by oneself in an ultimately supreme way. God's holiness also means that He has no contemporaries or rivals. He is so far above and beyond everyone and everything else. He is unreachable and unknowable, unless He chooses to reveal Himself to us. God's holiness also means that He is morally perfect and morally pure in every way and in relation to all of His other attributes. God's love is holy; His justice is holy; His mercy is holy; and so on and so forth. Everything about God transcends human knowledge and understanding. He is completely above, outside, and beyond all things. He is the origin of all things, and in Him alone all things hold together.

***

For I do not want you to be unaware, brothers, that our fathers were all under the cloud, and all passed through the sea, and all were baptized into Moses in the cloud and in the sea, and all ate the same spiritual food, and all drank the same spiritual drink. For they drank from the spiritual Rock that followed them, and the Rock was Christ. Nevertheless, with most of them God was not pleased, for they were overthrown in the wilderness. Now these things took place as examples for us, that we might not desire evil as they did.

1 Cor. 10:1-6

The holiness of God is immutable and unchangeable, and this can cause problems with human interaction. Moses, the man chosen to lead the Israelites out of Egypt, is regarded in Scripture as a hero of the faith. There are few spoken of like him in Scripture. He is held up as one of only a handful of men who walked and talked with God Himself. He is consistently pointed to as someone who pleased God and obeyed God, but when Moses disobeyed God and infringed on His holiness, His punishment was that he would not enter the Promised Land. By God's hand, Moses delivered his people from Egypt, led them through the wilderness for forty years, acted as God's ambassador, was given the Law of God on the mountainside to give to the people, and did everything that God asked of him. And in one moment of disobedience, he was denied entry into the Promised Land. Moses' life and story are documented in the books of Exodus, Leviticus, Numbers, and Deuteronomy.

Moses was upset with the Israelites and with good reason. Although God had provided for them, taken care of them, led them, and was about to lead them into the Promised Land, they grumbled and complained about everything; they were rebellious and ungrateful. They had come to a place where there was no water. So to once again show the people His glory, God commanded Moses to speak to the rock that was in the ground before him, and it would produce water for the people to drink. They continued complaining and grumbling, and this made Moses mad. So, instead of speaking to the rock, he struck it twice in anger. It produced water, but as a result of his disobedience, Moses was not allowed to enter the Promised Land.

At first glance, this might seem like a very severe punishment, but it only seems severe to us because we undervalue the holiness of God. We must remember that His judgments and His justice are also holy. It would seem that Moses also undervalued the holiness of God in that moment, and because God is so holy, the punishment fit the crime. This really was an act of unbelief before the people, so Moses received this penalty. "And the Lord said to Moses and Aaron, "Because you did not believe in me, to uphold me as holy in the eyes of the people of Israel, therefore you shall not bring this assembly into the land that I have given them" (Num. 20:12).

Later in the New Testament, the apostle Paul would identify this rock as a spiritual symbol of Christ, Who is our Rock that brings living water to His people. Although Moses couldn't have known what his disobedience was undermining at the time, it didn't matter. God's ways are higher than our ways, and this is an example of why we must obey Him even when we don't understand. Moses was called to save the Israelites, but his disobedience and imperfection also points to the need for a better Savior, a perfect Savior, a holy Savior. And this is something that could only be accomplished by God Himself.

We also see the demand for instant and severe justice when God's holiness was disrespected through disobedience in the story of Uzzah's death in 2 Samuel 6. The Ark of the Covenant was God's holy seat and was meant to be stored in the Holy of Holies, God's most holy place on the Earth. The Ark of the Covenant represented the manifest presence of God. It had been seized by the Philistines and kept as a trophy of their victory. But very quickly, they realized that their possession of the Ark was causing them much suffering, so they made arrangements to return it to Israel. They gave it back to Israel on a cart they had built for it.

In the Law of God, there was a very specific way God had commanded the Ark to be transported. According to God's instructions, the Ark was to be transported by the Kohathites by carrying it on poles that were run through rings that were on the Ark (Exod. 25:10-22; Num. 4:1-20). The Ark of the Covenant was the most holy representation of the glory of God on Earth. It was so holy that if anyone looked inside of it, they would die. Fifty thousand men were struck dead for looking into the Ark right before it was returned.

On the day the Ark was being returned to the holy place, everyone was very happy, and there was great celebration as they brought the Ark back. But instead of transporting the Ark in the way God commanded, they placed it on the newly built cart and had it pulled by oxen. And instead of having the people God instructed to bring it, two men who were volunteers brought back the Ark. One of these men, Uzzah, saw that one of the oxen lost its footing and the Ark began to slip, so he reached out to steady it and was instantly struck dead.

This seemed very severe to King David at first, and it made him fear the Lord—rightfully so. We should fear a holy God and realize that His glory and holiness will not be diminished for any reason; it cannot be. You can read this entire story in 2 Samuel 6:1-11.

We also see the holiness of God as displayed in the story of the prophet Isaiah's encounter with Him. God was going to use Isaiah in a very difficult time in Israel's history, so for Isaiah to speak on God's behalf, God gave him a revelation of His holiness. God would also use Isaiah to prophecy about Christ, the coming Messiah, so it was very important for Isaiah to be aware of God's holiness. Coming into contact with God's infinite holiness and moral perfection will always produce fear and reverence because we are sinful beings. The immediate response humanity has when exposed to God's perfection is awareness of our sin and fear because we also become aware that His perfect justice demands our destruction.

***

In the year that King Uzziah died I saw the Lord sitting upon a throne, high and lifted up; and the train of his robe filled the temple. Above him stood the seraphim. Each had six wings: with two he covered his face, and with two he covered his feet, and with two he flew. And one called to another and said: "Holy, holy, holy is the Lord of hosts; the whole earth is full of his glory!" And the foundations of the thresholds shook at the voice of him who called, and the house was filled with smoke. And I said: "Woe is me! For I am lost; for I am a man of unclean lips, and I dwell in the midst of a people of unclean lips; for my eyes have seen the King, the Lord of hosts!"

Isa. 6:1-5

In modern Christian culture, so many claim that they have come in contact with God; but honestly, if someone claims to know God and lacks fear and reverence for His holiness, I cannot believe them. It is impossible to taste the glory of God and to see even a small portion of His holiness and be the same. If we come away from an encounter with a holy God without being aware of our sin and without fear and reverence for God, we are deceived about Who God is.

***

"The fear of the LORD is the beginning of wisdom,
and the knowledge of the Holy One is insight."

Prov. 9:10

God is holy, and this is the greatest revelation of our lives as Christians. If we don't view God, this way we don't see or know the God of the Bible. We see all through the Old Testament displays of God's glory for the sake of His holy name. The greatest tragedy in the American church is the glorification of man at the expense of the glorification of God. God is holy, and His glory will not be rivaled; it can't be.

Throughout the Old Testament, we see the holiness of God displayed; but in the New Testament, we see the holiness of God revealed in the Person of Jesus Christ. We also see the love of God in the Gospel. We are wrong to believe that God in the New Testament is any less holy than He is in the Old Testament. The triune God is the same yesterday, today, and forever. God hates sin, and because He is holy, He can't leave sin unpunished because He is perfectly just. But because He loves us and is merciful, He extends undeserved grace to us through the sacrifice of His Son Jesus. Only God Himself was good enough to satisfy the justice and wrath His holiness and moral purity demanded.

I have heard people say that eternal damnation seems like an extreme punishment for rejecting the Gospel. This is a person who doesn't see the holiness of God. If you think spending eternity in Hell is too severe of a punishment for rejecting the sacrifice of Christ on the cross, it's because you over-value yourself and under-value Him. According to A.A. Hodge, "The holiness of God is not to be conceived of as one attribute among others. It is, rather, a general term representing the conception of God's consummate perfection and total glory. It is His infinite moral perfection crowning His infinite intelligence and power."

So, in regard to Jesus, Who is the physical representation of God Himself, it is right to say that rejection of Jesus is the ultimate rejection of

God's holiness. God literally owes us nothing, not even an explanation. But we, on the other hand, owe Him everything. He gave us life, and although we don't deserve it, has offered us forgiveness for our sins and eternal life with Him. We see in the Old Testament that God is so holy that any act of disobedience had very severe consequences, so how much more severe will judgement be for those who reject the sacrifice made by the Son of God Himself for undeserving sinners? The only proper response to the Gospel of Jesus Christ is unconditional surrender, repentance to God, and a commitment to live a life of worship and holiness in honor of Him and with allegiance toward Him.

PERSONAL HOLINESS

The idea of us living holy lives doesn't mean we are holy like God is holy or that we will ever be or ever could be. What it does mean is that in regeneration, we are changed and that in view of God's holiness, we strive to live a life of holiness in honor of and in service of Him. God calls us to be holy for the sake of His holiness. Living a life of personal holiness doesn't mean we are earning salvation. Salvation is an unearned gift from God. We are saved by grace alone, through faith alone, in Christ alone. Our life of holiness is lived in response to the free gift of salvation God has given us in the Gospel of Jesus Christ.

There are some that teach a heretical teaching that since we were made in God's image, we are little gods. I have heard false teachers say that everything in nature reproduces after its own kind, so when God said, "Let us make man in our image" (Gen. 1:26), this means that we are reproduced after the God kind. This is completely wrong. God is eternal, matchless, omnipresent, omniscient, and so many other things that we are not and will never be. God did create us in His image and likeness, but that is not the same thing as an animal or a human reproducing after its own kind. It is more like Someone far superior making something or building something. No matter how amazing the creation is, it is a mere creation of something far superior. God didn't merely make something out of materials that were laying around; He created something living out of nothing, and He created a universe out of nothing. Although humankind is an amazing creation of God, we are not in the same category as God, and to say otherwise is utterly heretical and wicked.

The reason I bring this heresy up in the chapter dealing with personal holiness is because I want to make sure that as I explain the biblical call to personal holiness, you understand I am not saying sinless perfection is possible. People often take this to a few different extremes. Some say we shouldn't worry about sin at all because we are like God, and once we are born again, we shouldn't expect to sin. If your faith is strong and your mind is right, you will be able to live in sinless perfection or some version of it.

Another branch on that same tree is the idea that we must work really hard not to sin, and to try hard to be accepted by God. And although most don't come out and say it, to them, it really comes down to doing more good than bad, which is what the Judaizers in the New Testament taught or what the Roman Catholic Church teaches. On the complete opposite side of the spectrum, there are people who believe that grace means it doesn't matter if we sin at all. God's grace is preached as a card or pass we receive, and that allows us to live any way we want. Any sort of expectation or call to personal holiness is called *legalism,* or working toward your salvation.

Here is what I believe the Bible teaches. We are saved by grace alone, through faith alone, in Christ alone. Salvation is completely an unearned gift from God. No character trait, no good deeds, no redeemable personal qualities, nothing in ourselves or of ourselves made us worthy of or in any way earned our salvation. Ephesians 2:8-10 says, "For by grace you have been saved through faith. And this is not your own doing; it is the gift of God, not a result of works, so that no one may boast. For we are his workmanship, created in Christ Jesus for good works, which God prepared beforehand, that we should walk in them."

So, we were not saved by our works in any way, shape, form, or fashion. We were saved simply because God chose to save us. But we were saved and reborn in Christ for the purpose of doing good works, which the Scripture says that God prepared beforehand for us to do. I don't want any confusion from anyone reading this. Our works and deeds, or even striving to live a holy life, has nothing to do with how God saved us or why God saved us. But in the life of a truly regenerate person, there will be good works, and there should be a life of holiness. Our works and our life of holiness doesn't save us, but I believe the Bible teaches that after conversion it is evidence that we are truly saved. That doesn't mean that we don't ever sin or even fall, but it does mean we love God and have a new nature in Christ. And when we sin and fall, we hate it and are convicted by the Holy Spirit of God living in us. A conviction that leads us to repentance. So, because we belong to and represent a holy God, we are called to be holy and set apart for His use and to bring Him glory in the Earth.

***

As obedient children, do not be conformed to the passions of your former ignorance, but as he who called you is holy, you also be holy in all your conduct, since it is written, "You shall be holy, for I am holy." And if you call on him as Father who judges impartially according to each one's deeds, conduct yourselves with fear throughout the time of your exile, knowing that you were ransomed from the futile ways inherited from your forefathers, not with perishable things such as silver or gold.

1 Peter 1:14-18

Peter doesn't tell us that we won't ever be tempted by the passions of our former ignorance. But he does remind us that we are called to be holy. God, through salvation, has caused the Holy Spirit to live inside of us, so we have been empowered to live a holy life. We don't ignore sin and pretend it isn't there; we overcome it by the power of the Holy Spirit. Having a casual attitude toward sin doesn't mean you are strong or mature or that you have a lot of faith; it shows you are prideful, immature, and foolish and that you don't value holiness or the God you serve very much.

Jonathan Edwards said, "A true and faithful Christian does not make holy living an accidental thing. It is his great concern. As the business of a soldier is to fight, so the business of the Christian is to be like Christ." Being like Christ in personal holiness should definitely be an outward thing, but initially and more importantly, it is an inward thing. We live holy lives because the Spirit of God lives in us and because we are reborn, hate sin, and fight sin. This is the core of self-denial because the flesh we are denying is corrupted by sin and full of sin.

***

"I am speaking in human terms, because of your natural limitations. For just as you once presented your members as slaves to impurity and to lawlessness leading to more lawlessness, so now present your members as slaves to righteousness leading to sanctification."

Rom. 6:19

We present our bodies and our lives to Christ in honor of Him. Out of knowledge and love for Christ, we flee from sin, knowing that sin leads to more sin. As we deny our sinful flesh and pursue holiness, we are sanctified. As I mentioned in a previous chapter, sanctification is a mysterious work of the Spirit, and although we know this is a work of God, we still must strive to live in obedience. The true evidence of the Spirit of God living in you is your desire for personal holiness and fellowship with God and a hatred and disdain for anything that conflicts with that.

We must remember that through sanctification and conforming to the image of Christ, we find holiness. Spiritual maturity in holiness isn't denying yourself of the wicked pleasures you once loved, it is not loving them anymore because through sanctification, you now love something else. The author of

Hebrews admonishes us, "Strive for peace with everyone, and for the holiness without which no one will see the Lord" (Heb. 12:14).

PRACTICAL HOLINESS

So often when we think of sin, we consider what things we call wrong or that our culture says are wrong. But the true standard for holiness comes from God, and we can find this standard in the Scriptures. True Christians often lacerate their souls because our culture—and sometimes, even our church—tells us something is acceptable that the Word of God and the Spirit of God living within us is telling us is not.

The word *legalism* is often used to discourage someone from biblical preaching and biblical living. This is the idea that we can take God's commands too seriously or that we are wrong when we hold someone else or even ourselves to the standard of God's Word. We are saved by grace, but a lack of desire to live in holiness and obedience toward the God Who saved us is showing a lack of love to that very God. There is a true legalism that is wrong, but it is wrong because it is unbiblical. It is putting conditions on people for salvation or in living lives of holiness that the Bible itself doesn't prescribe. If the Bible commands it, we should strive to do it; if the Bible forbids it, we should strive to live without it. Our love for God is best displayed in our obedience to God.

***

By this we know that we love the children of God, when we love God and obey his commandments. For this is the love of God, that we keep his commandments. And his commandments are not burdensome. For everyone who has been born of God overcomes the world. And this is the victory that has overcome the world—our faith.

1 John 5:2-4

Although there is a mysterious spiritual nature about the work of sanctification the Lord does in us, there is also a very practical and understandable application in relation to personal holiness. If you play in the mud, you will get dirty. That makes perfect sense, but on a heart and intention level, the question really becomes, do you want to get dirty? I believe that in sanctification, intentions of the heart are exposed. I also believe that in some cases, it exposes that maybe sanctification isn't occurring, which might be evidence that a person hasn't really been born again. So often we in the church try to give assurance of someone's salvation to them when honestly, only the Holy Spirit can do that. That is why we must fight sin as if it truly was our enemy and continue to examine ourselves in light of Scripture.

COME OUT FROM AMONG THEM

> Do not be unequally yoked with unbelievers. For what partnership has righteousness with lawlessness? Or what fellowship has light with darkness? What accord has Christ with Belial? Or what portion does a believer share with an unbeliever? What agreement has the temple of God with idols? For we are the temple of the living God; as God said, "I will make my dwelling among them and walk among them, and I will be their God, and they shall be my people. Therefore go out from their midst, and be separate from them, says the Lord, and touch no unclean thing; then I will welcome you, and I will be a father to you, and you shall be sons and daughters to me, says the Lord Almighty" (2 Cor. 6:14-18).

In the sixth chapter of Paul's second letter to the church of Corinth, he urges these young believers under inspiration of the Holy Spirit to be separated from the world. As the bride of Christ, we are called to keep ourselves pure, unstained, and unsoiled by the world as we wait for His return. Often today, we are told something completely opposite of this. We are told by the experiential, seek-friendly movement that to reach the world, we must be like the world. They use very worldly and pragmatic logic to come to this conclusion. We say, "Win the lost at all costs!" That sounds good as a slogan, but there is a cost that is too high and that God would never ask from us. God will never ask you to reach the lost at the expense of your personal holiness and your relationship with God.

The holiness of God is very important to God as is holiness of His people. Today, if you preach about living a life of personal holiness, you might be called legalistic. Honestly, when you preach God's Word and define what is right and wrong based on the words of Scripture, you might be called backward, outdated, and judgmental. The only real sin in American culture today is calling sin, sin. However, the words of Scripture plainly tell us that we are called to be separate, different, and even peculiar: "But ye are a chosen generation, a royal priesthood, a holy nation, a people for his own possession; that you may proclaim the excellencies of him who called you out of darkness into his marvelous light" (1 Peter 2:9).

We are meant to stand out, not to blend in. This is why in Matthew 5, we are told to be salt and light in this world. If we are reborn in Christ and living our lives according to Scripture, we will stand out because our lives will be countercultural, devout, self-sacrificing, Christ-centered, different, holy.

Often the reason why many reject the idea that we should strive for holiness is that they do come out of a truly legalistic background where there wasn't any room for people with outwardly sinful pasts to find acceptance in the body. Instead of being viewed as a new creature in Christ, they were rejected and viewed by their past instead of through the lens of their repentance and new life in Christ. This is absurd because all were sinners and in desperate need for the grace of God. Typically, it is because we rate past sins based on how society perceives them. There is no sin too great or grievous that it can't be washed away by the blood of Jesus. But in response to this and in an effort not to be perceived as legalistic and judgmental, we have swung the pendulum far in the other direction. The grace of God and living devout and holy lives is not at odds with each other; in fact, it is because of the grace of God that we are able to live a life that is holy and pleasing to God.

***

For if we have been united with him in a death like his, we shall certainly be united with him in a resurrection like his. We know that our old self was crucified with him in order that the body of sin might be brought to nothing, so that we would no longer be enslaved to sin. For one who has died has been set free from sin. Now if we have died with Christ, we believe that we will also live with him. We know that Christ, being raised from the dead, will never die again; death no longer has dominion over him. For the death he died he died to sin, once for all, but the life he lives he lives to God.

Rom. 6:5-10

It's through the grace of God given to us in the Gospel that we are able to crucify our flesh and overcome the sin that once mastered us and to live holy lives. In much of the evangelical church today, we are so afraid of being called judgmental that many are willing to endure all sorts of wickedness in the house of God. We don't bat an eye at professed Christians living together when they are not married. Pornography and drunkenness are just norms today. We love entertainment that is vile, full of blasphemy, sexual immorality, sorcery, and every kind of idolatry. We claim to be married to God but are having an unashamed and open affair with the world. You cannot live like the world and love the world and still love God. In fact, we are commanded in 1 John 2:15-17:

> Do not love the world or the things in the world. If anyone loves the world, the love of the Father is not in him. For all that is in the world—the desires of the flesh and the desires of the eyes and pride of life—is not from the Father but is from the world. And the world is passing away along with its desires, but whoever does the will of God abides forever.

COME OUT FROM AMONG THE WORLD FOR THE GLORY OF GOD

Paul tells the church in Corinth that since we have been chosen by God, we must come out from among them and be separate for the glory of God. Worshiping the Lord and living lives that bring God glory is the highest purpose of our lives as Christians. We were chosen by God and belong to God, and that should be apparent in all our words and in all of our deeds. Remember what it says in 1 Peter 2:9: we should be holy and declare His praises because He has brought us "out of darkness into his marvelous light."

So, if we are supposed to be separate from unbelievers, how can we do that and still be in this world? And how do we reconcile that with the Great Commission?

> And Jesus came and said to them, "All authority in heaven and on earth has been given to me. Go therefore and make disciples of all nations, baptizing them in the name of the Father and of the Son and of the Holy Spirit, teaching them to observe all that I have commanded you. And behold, I am with you always, to the end of the age" (Matt. 28:18-20).

First, it is important to make the distinction that separation and isolation is not the same thing. We are to live in the world but not be of the world. God isn't calling us to hide from the world, to build a monastery somewhere and never see anyone. But in a very real and practical way, we are to lead separate lives and abstain from the evil in the world and strictly and devoutly live our lives according to the Scripture as those who don't want to become stained by the world.

Let's look at this practically according to 2 Corinthians 6:14. "Do not be yoked together with unbelievers!" This means you shouldn't date unbelievers; you shouldn't have unbelievers in your inner circle; and you shouldn't get counsel or advice from unbelievers. Paul poses a rhetorical question here: For what does righteousness and wickedness have in common? The answer should be nothing! What harmony is there between Christ and the devil? None! What does a believer have in common with an unbeliever? Nothing! And if you do, it says something about your walk with God. Non-believers have no relevant advice for us. How could they? Everything about the life of a believer should be different.

What fellowship can light have with darkness? We cannot fellowship with darkness. That doesn't mean we are rude or mean or that we do not talk to unbelievers. We should be the friendliest and kindest people around. Fellowship means to spend time together and to allow them into our lives as close friends—the kind of relationships where you advise them and they advise you, a relationship where they speak into your life and impact decisions you make. Your fellowship should be with likeminded Christians who build you up in the faith and who you build up in the faith—fellowship that is full of God's love and truth, fellowship that holds each other accountable to holiness, righteousness, and living a life according to God's Word.

That doesn't mean we don't have friendships of any kind with lost loved ones, but all relationships with unbelievers should be thought of as evangelistic in nature. You might say, "I love these people, so that doesn't seem fair." That is one reason you must live a holy and separated life and be evangelistic in interactions with lost people whom you love because they need to see you walking out your faith. They need to see a life that follows the Gospel you preach. If they are outside of Christ, no matter how good they are and no matter how much you love them, they are going to die and go to Hell without Christ. They desperately need to see the light of Christ being lived out in your life. Being like them, acting like them, doing worldly things like them doesn't draw them to a holy God; it merely misrepresents Him and pushes them further into darkness.

But ultimately, you must live unyoked from the world and separate from unbelievers because this is what a holy God commands of you. If we are in Christ, we are God's temple, and we must not defile God's temple. We are indwelled by the Spirit of God, and while it's true that our salvation isn't based on our performance but on what Christ has done, we cannot expect to live in sin and experience the power and presence of God. God not only forgave us of our sin, but He also now calls us His children. And as His children, we must obey Him.

***

Therefore, preparing your minds for action, and being sober-minded, set your hope fully on the grace that will be brought to you at the revelation of Jesus Christ. As obedient children, do not be conformed to the passions of your former ignorance, but as he who called you is holy, you also be holy in all your conduct, since it is written, "You shall be holy, for I am holy."

1 Peter 1:13-16

Peter doesn't say you won't ever have evil desires; he says do not conform to evil desires like you did when you lived in ignorance. When you were in the dark, you didn't know any better; but now that you are in the light of the Lord, you are alive and aware of God because your spiritual eyes have been opened to the truth.

One reason we don't care much about personal holiness and keeping ourselves pure and clean in reverence of a holy God is because there is not much reverence for God in our culture. Honestly, there's not much reverence for God in much of the church. Why is this? It's because we don't fear the Lord, and we don't fear the Lord because we don't know the Lord. To truly know the God of the Bible is to fear Him and to have reverence for Him. The salvific promises of God are for the people of God, and those who belong to God will live holy lives because of true knowledge of the Lord.

***

"Since we have these promises, beloved, let us cleanse ourselves from every defilement of body and spirit, bringing holiness to completion in the fear of God."

2 Cor. 7:1

When reading the Bible—or really, when reading anything—when you come across the word *therefore*, a great rule of thumb is to go back before to see what the *therefore* is there for. That's kind of a silly way to put it, but it's true. In the English Standard Version of 2 Corinthians 7:1, *therefore* is replaced with *since*, but the principle is the same. So, what is the therefore there for? To remind us what God said to us in the previous verses:

> What agreement has the temple of God with idols? For we are the temple of the living God; as God said, "I will make my dwelling among them and walk among them, and I will be their God, and they shall be my people. Therefore go out from their midst, and be separate from them, says the Lord, and touch no unclean thing; then I will welcome you, and I will be a father to you, and you shall be sons and daughters to me, says the Lord Almighty" (2 Cor. 6:16-18).

We should live lives of personal holiness because God says that He will be our God, and we will be His people. So, because of this wonderful promise, we should come out from among the world and be separate. We live holy lives because we are sons and daughters of God Himself. What an incomparable blessing to be part of the family of God. God says, "Touch no unclean thing; then I will welcome you." Self-denial of things that are sinful, unclean, and wicked for the sake of fellowship with God shows that worship of God and fellowship with God is the greatest desire of your heart. Personal holiness doesn't earn us anything; it merely exposes what is truly in our hearts.

***

Then Jesus told his disciples, "If anyone would come after me, let him deny himself and take up his cross and follow me. For whoever would save his life will lose it, but whoever loses his life for my sake will find it. For what will it profit a man if he gains the whole world and forfeits his soul? Or what shall a man give in return for his soul?"

Matt. 16:24-26

Deny yourself, be holy, and be set apart. We are set apart for God's holy purposes; and we are also set apart from chasing the things of this world, chasing what everyone one else is chasing, because we have already found our treasure. This world is rapidly passing away, and if you love the world and the things in this world, you will perish with this world. If you try to argue with the biblical idea of pursuing holiness because God loves you, I'm not questioning God's love toward you, but I am questioning your love toward God—a God Who gave you life, a God Who offered mercy instead of judgment and grace instead of damnation. We live set-apart lives because we love God and live our lives in view of God's love and mercy toward us. Remember, holy in our case doesn't mean perfect. No one is perfect, but we can use that as an excuse to trample the very grace by which God saved us, as we see in Hebrews 10:

> For if we go on sinning deliberately after receiving the knowledge of the truth, there no longer remains a sacrifice for sins, but a fearful expectation of judgment, and a fury of fire that will consume the adversaries. Anyone who has set aside the law of Moses dies without mercy on the evidence of two or three witnesses. How much worse punishment, do you think, will be deserved by the one who has trampled underfoot the Son of God, and has profaned the blood of the covenant by which he was sanctified, and has outraged the Spirit of grace? For we know him who said, "Vengeance is mine; I will repay." And again, "The Lord will judge his people." It is a fearful thing to fall into the hands of the living God (Heb. 10:26-31).

God will judge His people, and we will give account for the way we lived this life. If we claim to have been saved by grace but live in a way that treats Christ's sacrifice with contempt, it shows the truth about our hearts, and the Scripture says we should be worried. Remember, there is nothing done in the darkness that will not one day be brought to light.

HOLINESS IS EVIDENCE WE ARE LIGHT

"Again Jesus spoke to them, saying, 'I am the light of the world.
Whoever follows me will not walk in darkness, but will have the light of life.'"

John 8:12

Personal holiness in our lives is evidence that the Spirit of Christ is truly living inside of us. Jesus is the Light of the world, and in salvation, through the indwelling of the Holy Spirit, that Light lives in us. This is why Jesus said to us in Matthew 5:

> "You are the light of the world. A city set on a hill cannot be hidden. Nor do people light a lamp and put it under a basket, but on a stand, and it gives light to all in the house. In the same way, let your light shine before others, so that they may see your good works and give glory to your Father who is in heaven" (Matt. 5:14-16).

Jesus brought light and life to a lost and dark world. Jesus fulfilled the Law and every Old Testament prophecy that foretold of His coming. Scripture says through one man, Adam, came sin and death, and through one Man, Jesus Christ, came life and restoration to God. Without Him, we lived in darkness, in spiritual death and spiritual blindness, the entire world was completely hopeless. We had no way to God, and without God opening our eyes, we actually had no way to even know that we needed God. That is an all-consuming and damming darkness. The saddest part is that those who are blind cannot truly even perceive how dark the darkness really is. But in the Gospel, our eyes are opened to the darkness, and we see how grave our situation is and how lost we really are. Then we see Jesus, the Light of the world—a blinding Light that exposes our sin and need—and through repentance, we find forgiveness. This same holy God takes up residence in us.

Through the prophet Isaiah in the Old Testament, the coming Messiah was foretold to be a light to all nations: "'I am the LORD; I have called you in righteousness; I will take you by the hand and keep you; I will give you as a covenant for the people, a light for the nations" (Isa. 42:6).

Then in John 12:46, Jesus refers to Himself as the Light that was referred to in Isaiah. The sovereign and holy God of the Old Testament Who reigns in unapproachable light, Who said Abram would become the father of many nations, Who gave the Law of God to Moses, Who struck Uzzah in 2 Samuel, Who filled the temple with His glory is the Son of God, Jesus Christ, and death and darkness have no power over Him. "In him is life, and the life was the light of men. The light shines in the darkness, and the darkness has not overcome it" (John 1:4-5). The glory of God has been revealed to us in the person of Christ, and "[His] word is a lamp to [our] feet and a light to [our] path" (Psalm 119:105). The light of God revealed to us in the Gospel. A holy God Who knew no wrong took on flesh and suffered in our place, endured and overcame death, and rose from the dead so that we could be delivered from death and darkness and brought into His marvelous light and eternal life.

***

"That the Christ must suffer and that, by being the first to rise from the dead, he would proclaim light both to the our people and to the Gentiles."

Acts 26:23

Jesus was the first to proclaim light to the nation, but He was not the last. We are called to be light in a dark and hopeless world. Jesus says that in regeneration, we "are the light of the world[,] a city set on a hill" (Matt. 5:14). Not to be hidden but to stand out. We are sons and daughters of Light, so we must be separate in our ways, holy in our lives, and unified in the message of the cross. Through our proclaiming His Gospel and living holy and devout lives, we are used by the Holy Spirit to draw the sheep of God to Jesus Christ. If Christ is truly living in us, we have His life and His light living in and shining through us.

Salt and light are forged in us through persecution and through suffering as we become more and more like Christ. The world hates holiness, and the world hates light. So, if you truly are these things, the world will hate you. You can't live in the light if you still love darkness. John 3:19-21 tells us:

> And this is the judgment: the light has come into the world, and people loved the darkness rather than the light because their works were evil. For everyone who does wicked things hates the light and does not come to the light, lest his works should be exposed. But whoever does what is true comes to the light, so that it may be clearly seen that his works have been carried out in God.

Our purpose in life as followers of Christ is to worship the holy God in spirit and in truth, to bring glory to the holy God in every area of our lives, to make disciples as commanded by the holy God, and to conform to the image of the holy God. To be holy as He is holy.

CHAPTER 9

THE SUFFICIENCY OF SCRIPTURE

For the word of God is living and active, sharper than any two-edged sword,
piercing to the division of soul and of spirit, of joints and of marrow,
and discerning the thoughts and intentions of the heart. And no creature
is hidden from his sight, but all are naked and exposed to the eyes of him
to whom we must give account.

Heb. 4:12-13

As a follower of Christ in a world that loves darkness and sin and stands opposed to God, it is very important to know what ground is solid and unfailing and to what we can hold fast. For us as Christ followers, that solid ground is the Scripture. Many people are willing to say that they believe in the inerrancy of Scripture, which is good, but most in the church don't view the Scripture as sufficient. If they did, we would see a lot less gimmicks and manmade methods and a lot more Gospel proclamation and expository preaching. The two most important things we have in this life as disciples of Jesus are the Spirit of God and the Word of God.

THE SPIRIT OF GOD

There is no greater gift than the gift of the Holy Spirit. The Holy Spirit is God, the third Person of the triune Godhead. The Spirit has many functions and roles in the world and also in the life of the believer. It is the Holy Spirit Who convicts us of our sin and draws us to repentance.

***

Nevertheless, I tell you the truth: it is to your advantage that I go away, for

if I do not go away, the Helper will not come to you. But if I go, I will send

him to you. And when he comes, he will convict the world concerning sin and

righteousness and judgment: concerning sin, because they do not believe in

me; concerning righteousness, because I go to the Father, and you will see me

no longer; concerning judgment, because the ruler of this world is judged.

John 16:7-11

It is through regeneration we respond to the conviction of the Holy Spirit regarding our sin and are saved. In salvation, we are sealed with the Spirit, which is a confirmation of God's pledge that we are His children and that He will save us from judgment in the end. This is very important because without the Spirit of Christ living in us, we do not belong to God. This is one reason why the Gospel must be the focal point of all we do as disciples. Without the Gospel, there can be nothing else, and honestly, nothing else matters.

Jesus also said that the Spirit of God would be our Comforter, our Helper, and our Guide. In John 14, Jesus said that He was going back to the Father but that it was better for us that He did because He promised to send the Helper, which is another name for the Spirit: "And I will ask the Father, and he will give you another Helper, to be with you forever" (John 14:16).

It's through the Spirit of God that we bear outward fruit as evidence of who we are inside and of the sanctifying work God the Spirit is doing in us. This evidence will manifest in our lives with a spiritual harvest of "love, joy, peace, patience, kindness, goodness, faithfulness, gentleness, self-control" (Gal. 5:22-23). The Spirit of God will also equip us with spiritual gifts as He sees fit, meant for edifying the body of Christ and forwarding the Gospel of Jesus Christ in the Earth (1 Cor. 12). But Jesus also said the Spirit of God will be the Revealer of truth, namely the truth of God's Word. One of the Holy Spirit's main functions in the life of a believer is to help us understand and interpret God's Word. Jesus told His disciples, "When the Spirit of truth comes, he will guide you into all the truth, for he will not speak on his own authority, but whatever he hears he will speak, and he will declare to you the things that are to come" (John 16:13).

It is through the Word of God that the Spirit leads us into all truth in regard to proper worship, doctrine, and living as disciples of Jesus. The Spirit opens our eyes and helps us perceive the truth of God's Word and enables us to walk it out. God's greatest revelation comes to us through the Spirit of God, and His greatest revelation is that Jesus Christ is Who He claimed to be: eternal God, Son of God, the Messiah. We can find this revelation in the sacred, inerrant words of Scripture.

THE WORD OF GOD

When we talk about the sufficiency of Scripture, we are saying that Scripture is sufficient in that it is the only inspired, inerrant, and, therefore, final authority for Christians for faith and godliness, with all other authorities being subservient to Scripture. I have heard people argue against this point in subtle and even in very direct ways. Often, people who are obsessed with signs, wonders, and manifestations think that this view of the Bible is too restrictive. I heard a pastor who is famous for his teachings on healings, signs, and wonders once say, "We believe in the Father, Son and the Holy Spirit, not the Father, Son and the Holy Bible." What a foolish and unnecessary thing to say, unless you sought to undermine the authority of Scripture. The Spirit of Truth and the Word of Truth will never contradict or undermine each other. He is perfect, and so is His Word. "All Scripture is breathed out by God and profitable for teaching, for reproof, for correction, and for training in righteousness, that the man of God may be complete, equipped for every good work" (2 Tim. 3:16-17).

The Bible is God's eternal and established Word. The Scripture is God's unified, consistent, and primary means of speaking to us and leading us into all truth. All other things are subject to the authority of God's Word.

This is why it is constantly under attack by people outside the church and, more dangerously, by people inside the church. If we truly view Scripture as God's authoritative Word, then we will subject everything else to it. If we are truly Christians, that means that we have come to terms with the fact that we have been corrupted by sin, and once saved, we are in the process of being sanctified, conformed, and transformed into the image of Christ. So, how foolish is it for us to think we can rightfully judge what is right and wrong without the Word of Truth? How much more foolish is it to believe we can make moral judgements about the righteousness and justice of God and His Word?

When we try to judge the validity of God's Word with secondary or outside sources, we are setting those things up as the judge of God Himself, which shows that we don't really believe in God. You cannot reject the Scriptures and be a Christian! I'm not saying that misunderstanding a detail of the Bible means you are not a Christian, or that you must have an exhaustive knowledge of the Bible to be saved, or that true Christians do not disagree on many secondary issues. I am saying that you cannot willfully reject something the Bible clearly teaches. I have studied the Bible for years, and there are many subjects and doctrines that I don't fully understand, even ones about which I have been wrong and about which I later changed my mind. But the true Christian knows that God's Word is true and established and unchanging and that even if we don't completely understand it all, we accept it as completely true and authoritative as we humbly study and seek to know God.

In the book of Psalms, there are many places where God's Word is mentioned. The longest chapter in the entire Bible, Psalm 119, speaks about how great and powerful the Word of God is. It's interesting to me that the longest chapter in the entire Bible is praising the benefits and describing the value of His Word. All through the Psalms, there is reflection on and praise of the Law of the Lord and His holy precepts. Psalm 19 also talks about the Law of the Lord and gives a poetic and prophetic description of God's precious and perfect Word:

> The law of the Lord is perfect, reviving the soul; the testimony of the Lord is sure, making wise the simple; the precepts of the Lord are right, rejoicing the heart; the commandment of the Lord is pure, enlightening the eyes; the fear of the Lord is clean, enduring forever; the rules of the Lord are true, and righteous altogether. More to be desired are they than gold, even much fine gold; sweeter also than honey and drippings of the honeycomb. Moreover, by them is your servant warned; in keeping them there is great reward. Who can discern his errors? Declare me innocent from hidden faults. Keep back your servant also from presumptuous sins; let them not have dominion over me! Then I shall be blameless, and innocent of great transgression. Let the words of my mouth and the meditation of my heart be acceptable in your sight, O Lord, my rock and my redeemer (Psalm 19:7-14).

In the Scripture, we have the full counsel of God and everything that we need for "life and godliness" (2 Peter 1:3). God reveals Himself in this psalm and throughout the Old Testament in ways that are prophetic and timeless. In Psalm 19:7-14, we see how God works through His Word in the lives of believers and in the world at large. This psalm says so much. By the Scripture, we are warned to keep from harm, and it says for those who keep God's Word, "there is great reward." His decrees are firm and righteous and unfailing.

The Scriptures are directly from God Himself. If you can't take God at His Word, you can't have saving faith. The Bible is self-identified all throughout the Scripture as the Word of God. If some parts are inspired while other parts are not, how can you trust any of it? You can't. And who gets to decide what parts are reliable and what parts are not? You? Me? Some other mere created being? Either we trust God, or we don't. It's all tied together. If you can believe in the Gospel; a virgin birth; the sinless life of Christ; His literal death, resurrection, and ascension into Heaven, then you are deceived if you say you can't believe His Word has been preserved for us. The Bible is true, reliable, and perfect; and it is the final word in the life of a Christian.

> And how from childhood you have been acquainted with the sacred writings, which are able to make you wise for salvation through faith in Christ Jesus. All Scripture is breathed out by God and profitable for teaching, for reproof, for correction, and for training in righteousness, that the man of God may be complete, equipped for every good work (2 Tim. 3:15-17).

Believing that the Bible is God's Word and inerrant is one thing, but saying that is it sufficient is another altogether. Do we believe that the Scriptures are sufficient and powerful? If the evangelical church in America truly believed that, our churches wouldn't be overrun with church consulting groups, secular gimmicks, and the powerless methods of men. Our churches would be filled with biblical theology instead of secular psychology. Pastors ziplining to the stage, sermon series based on worldly movies, high production entertainment with a dash of Scriptural validation—please explain to me how someone can use worldly methods and say that they really believe that the Word of God is powerful and sufficient? I don't think anyone honestly can. What we desperately need are men who fear the Lord, reverence the Scripture, and boldly and fearlessly preach the Word.

✳✳✳

"Your word is a lamp to my feet and a light to my path."

Psalm 119:105

Often, I hear people subtly try to undermine the Bible by saying that the Spirit of God lives in them and leads them. While this statement can be true, the problem is this: none of us this side of eternity are fully sanctified, so we are imperfect. And while I am not debating the fact that the Spirit lives and moves in the life of the believer, we can be deceived, misled, and flat out wrong. But the Bible is never wrong! Psalm 19 says that it is perfect and clean and enlightening. Your thoughts won't always be true. Your feelings will mislead you, and this world will deceive you. But the Word of God is established forever; it will never fail, never fade, and never change. It contains everything we need for life and godliness; it is inerrant, authoritative, and sufficient!

***

"Forever, O LORD, Your word is firmly fixed in the heavens."

Psalm 119:89

God's Word is set in Heaven forever! That is something on which we can rely. If you are saved, the Spirit of God does live in you, but the flesh is weak and imperfect. Many times when people argue this way, it is because there is something in the Bible that can't be reconciled with their life, and so, they try to put the Spirit and the Word at odds with each other. They believe this is a position that can't be argued. But the truth is if what you claim the Spirit says is in opposition with what the Bible teaches, then it is not the Spirit of God. If it is a spirit, it's not the Holy Spirit; but more often than not, it is your feelings. Your feelings are not the Holy Spirit of God! The Spirit of Truth will never contradict the Word of Truth, so what is the solution? Submit to the Bible in all things.

SEEKING SOUND DOCTRINE

The heavens declare the glory of God, and the sky above proclaims his handiwork. Day to day pours out speech, and night to night reveals knowledge. There is no speech, nor are there words, whose voice is not heard. Their voice goes out through all the earth, and their words to the end of the world. In them he has set a tent for the sun, which comes out like a bridegroom leaving his chamber, and, like a strong man, runs its course with joy. Its rising is from the end of the heavens, and its circuit to the end of them, and there is nothing hidden from its heat. The law of the Lord is perfect, reviving the soul; the testimony of the Lord is sure, making wise the simple; the precepts of the Lord are right, rejoicing the heart; the commandment of the Lord is pure, enlightening the eyes (Psalm 19:1-8).

All of Psalm 19 and all 176 verses of Psalm 119 are validating the Word of God as valuable and perfect in every possible way, and it is the Spirit of God living in the follower of Jesus that not only opens their eyes to this but also empowers them to walk it out. Anyone who tries to make you question the established Word of the sovereign Lord is from the evil one. The devil has been doing this since the very beginning of time. When God created the first man, Adam, He blessed him and created a lush and beautiful garden for him, and He told him that it was all for him to govern and enjoy. God told him that he could eat from any of the trees in the garden except for the one that was in the middle of the garden. God warned him that if he ate from this tree, he would surely die.

> Now the serpent was more crafty than any other beast of the field that the Lord God had made. He said to the woman, "Did God actually say, 'You shall not eat of any tree in the garden'?" And the woman said to the serpent, "We may eat of the fruit of the trees in the garden, but God said, 'You shall not eat of the fruit of the tree that is in the midst of the garden, neither shall you touch it, lest you die.'" But the serpent said to the woman, "You will not surely die. For God knows that when you eat of it your eyes will be opened, and you will be like God, knowing good and evil." So when the woman saw that the tree was good for food, and that it was a delight to the eyes, and that the tree was to be desired to make one wise, she took of its fruit and ate, and she also gave some to her husband who was with her, and he ate. Then the eyes of both were opened, and they knew that they were naked. And they sewed fig leaves together and made themselves loincloths (Gen. 3:1-7).

The devil, in the form of a serpent, came to Eve and got her to question God's Word: "Did God really say"? He got her to question God's Word by questioning His intentions and goodness. She ate the forbidden fruit and convinced her husband to as well, and sin and death were brought into the world. God's Word is established, and what He says is ironclad and will always come to pass. This is still the devil's tactics today. The decrees of God in Scripture are reliable, unchanging, unfailing, and authoritative. Anything or anyone that tries to make you question the integrity of God's Word is of the devil, plain and simple. It doesn't matter if they have a Christian television show, if they write books, if they are famous, if they are your family or your dearest friend. If they try to undermine the authority of, bring doubt to, or question the reliability of Scripture, they are being used by the evil one, even if they don't realize it.

***

And then the lawless one will be revealed, whom the Lord will kill with the breath of his mouth and bring to nothing by the appearance of his coming. The coming of the lawless one is by the activity of Satan with all power and false signs and wonders, and with all wicked deception for those who are perishing, because they refused to love the truth and so be saved.

2 Thess. 2:8-10

We are at the point where much of our culture is Christian in name only. One thing that separates true Christians from false converts is the love of the truth. God is Truth, and because of this, His Word is truth. As we move closer to the end, this will be more prevalent and out in the open. Eventually, a figure called "the lawless one" will appear, and he will come with power and signs and false wonders and will deceive many who will think that they are saved, but they will not be because they didn't receive love for the truth.

Those who love the truth will be saved because those who love the truth also love Jesus. If you claim to love Jesus but do not love and cherish His saving Word, then you might be one of those deceived by wickedness. This Scripture right here should be enough to make you realize that signs and wonders are not necessarily an indication of what is true and from God, but the Word of Truth is. People who are obsessed with signs and wonders are easily deceived, but those who love truth will not be.

Our culture, even much of American church culture, hates the word *doctrine*. I've heard people say things like, "I don't care about doctrine, but I love Jesus." This is absurd and idiotic. That would be like telling your wife that you love her, but you don't care about what she has to say or calling yourself a law-abiding citizen as you're robbing a bank. Sinful, unregenerate hearts don't love the truth, but they still want to feel like they are all right with God. So, to validate their compromise, they need people pretending to be pastors to tell them what they want to hear. Sound doctrine divides! It divides sheep from goats, true disciples from false converts, lovers of truth from lovers of sin. Doctrine comes from the righteous decrees of the Lord, which are given to us in His Word.

***

I charge you in the presence of God and of Christ Jesus, who is to judge the living and the dead, and by his appearing and his kingdom: preach the word; be ready in season and out of season; reprove, rebuke, and exhort, with complete patience and teaching. For the time is coming when people will not endure sound teaching, but having itching ears they will accumulate for themselves teachers to suit their own passions, and will turn away from listening to the truth and wander off into myths. As for you, always be sober-minded, endure suffering, do the work of an evangelist, fulfill your ministry.

2 Tim. 4:1-5

When the apostle Paul was in prison awaiting execution, he wrote what is probably the last epistle he ever penned, 2 Timothy. This was a letter to his son in the faith, Timothy, whom he loved. In some of the final words of his life, Paul urged Timothy above all else to preach the Word! He didn't say to be relevant and preach to people's felt needs or try not to offend anyone so the church would grow. He tells Timothy to preach the Word of God when it's well received and when it's not, when it's popular and when it's not.

The job of a truth-loving, biblical preacher is to preach the Word and use it to correct, rebuke, and encourage as you disciple men and women whom God has entrusted to your care. It's so important because you won't be the only kind of preacher that exists. There will also be preachers who don't biblically rebuke or correct; instead, they only encourage people as they preach them toward destruction. These preachers will be raised up by the masses who are on the broad road "that leads to destruction" (Matt. 7:13) and who hate the truth and reject sound doctrine. So, they surround themselves with false teachers who say what their itching ears want to hear. Both parties are filling a need for the other. The false convert needs someone to validate their compromise, sin, greed, and rebellious heart. The false teacher is looking for fools who will enrich, empower, and validate their heresy. Both parties lie to each other, soothe each other's seared and calloused consciences, and validate each other's deception as truth. The true, biblical preacher will be hated by them because he loves the truth and boldly speaks the truth. Amos 5:10 says, "They hate him who reproves in the gate, and they abhor him who speaks the truth" (Amos 5:10).

Sound doctrine is the truth and is exclusively revealed to us in the Word of God. Those who love God love His Word, and those who say they love God but despise any part of His Word are liars. The sound doctrine of God's Word reveals to us Jesus, shows us the way to be saved, tells us how to live as Christians, demonstrates how to properly worship, reveals to us the promises of God to the believer for salvation, and unveils the promise of destruction to those who do not belong to Him.

JESUS REVEALED BY THE WORD AS THE WORD

In the beginning was the Word, and the Word was with God, and the Word
was God. He was in the beginning with God. All things were made through
him, and without him was not any thing made that was made. In him was life,
and the life was the light of men. The light shines in the darkness,
and the darkness has not overcome it.

John 1:1-5

In the first chapter of the apostle John's gospel, he gives an account of the beginning that sounds a lot like the Genesis Creation account. In Genesis 1:1, it says, "In the beginning, God created the heavens and the earth." John references the same event, but in his account, he says, "In the beginning was the Word, and the Word was with God, and the Word was God" (John 1:1). Genesis 1:26 says, "Then God said, 'Let us make man in our image, after our likeness." So, the Word was there in the Creation story with God. And John takes this one step further by saying that not only was the Word in the creation story, but also the Word *was* God. He attributes all creation to Him and says, "Without Him was not any thing made that was made" (John 1:3).

***

"And the Word became flesh and dwelt among us, and we have seen his glory,
glory as of the only Son from the Father, full of grace and truth."

John 1:14

The Word that "became flesh," the Light that overcomes darkness (John 1:5), the One Who is full of grace and truth (John 1:14) is Jesus. Jesus Himself is God's Word, Who came to Earth and took on flesh. God fulfilled His Word with His Word and revealed Himself through His Word. God saved us with His Word. The eternal Son was present at Creation; He always has been and always will be because, like God the Father and God the Holy Spirit, Jesus is God. Jesus is eternal and trustworthy because He is the Word. In the pages of the sacred Scripture, Christ is revealed to us. The entire Bible is about Jesus

Christ. Through the Law and Prophets, we are shown foreshadowing of God, but it is clear right from the beginning that we need a better Man than Adam; we need a better Savior than Moses; we need a better King than David; and we need a better Sacrifice than animals.

The gospel of John is very different from the synoptic gospels, Matthew, Mark, and Luke. The word *synoptic* just means "similar." John is definitely different—not in the Gospel he presents, but in the way it is structured and the way it is presented to us. John seems to want us to be awestruck right from the beginning of the book. The Lamb of God Who takes away the sin of the world is God Himself. So, as you read through John's gospel, you can't help but be humbled and reverent because the mystery of all things is revealed to us right in the beginning. The same God Who spoke the world into existence also took on human flesh and died for us.

I believe that John called Jesus "the Word" because he saw Jesus as Truth and because he realized that His words brought about creation and salvation. John documented Peter's words when he acknowledged that Jesus had the words of life.

***

"Simon Peter answered him, 'Lord, to whom shall we go?
You have the words of eternal life.'"

John 6:68

But John makes it clear that Jesus not only had the words of life but that He also *is* the Word of life. They had to follow Him because He is the Way to salvation. He is Truth; He is light; He is Life; and He is God! From eternity past to infinity future, Jesus Christ is the incorruptible, inerrant, authoritative, and sufficient Word of God; and He is the same yesterday, today, and forever. He is revealed to us perfectly and clearly in the Scripture.

***

"I am coming soon. Hold fast what you have, so that no one may seize your
crown. The one who conquers, I will make him a pillar in the temple of my
God. Never shall he go out of it, and I will write on him the name of my God,
and the name of the city of my God, the new Jerusalem, which comes down
from my God out of heaven, and my own new name. He who has an ear, let
him hear what the Spirit says to the churches."

Rev. 3:11-13

John the apostle also wrote the book of Revelation, and in that book, John gives a description of the resurrected Christ that is mind-blowing. He goes to very great lengths to describe how majestic and radiant Jesus is. How beautiful and also terrifying it will be to see the glorious perfection of the King of all kings and the Lord of all lords. John says, "His eyes are like a flame of fire, and on his head are many diadems . . . He is clothed in a robe dipped in blood, and the name by which he is called is The Word of God" (Rev. 19:12-13). Jesus is the Word of God! To deny God's Word is to deny the Savior. To have a low view of Scripture is to have a low view of God. As Christian disciples, we must realize that there is nothing above God and there is no decree that could be above His Word. One of Christ's names is the Word of God, and we will be judged by Him according to that Word.

CHRIST REVEALED IN THE SCRIPTURE IS ENOUGH

Long ago, at many times and in many ways, God spoke to our fathers by the prophets, but in these last days he has spoken to us by his Son, whom he appointed the heir of all things, through whom also he created the world. He is the radiance of the glory of God and the exact imprint of his nature, and he upholds the universe by the word of his power. After making purification for sins, he sat down at the right hand of the Majesty on high, having become as much superior to angels as the name he has inherited is more excellent than theirs (Heb. 1:1-4).

Jesus, as revealed in the Scripture, is the final Word and God's final revelation to us. To look beyond Him is saying what He has accomplished isn't enough. The fulfillment of all Scripture, all Law, all prophecy, and the salvation of His elect is found in Him alone. When we desperately look for miracles to validate Jesus beyond resurrection from the dead, which is what regeneration is, we show our lack of understanding and our lack of value for the cross. There is nothing more beautiful and valuable than Jesus, and there is nothing more amazing than the Gospel—the death, burial, and resurrection of Jesus Himself. God has revealed Himself in Christ, and Christ has revealed Himself to us in the Word.

THE POWER OF THE SCRIPTURE

Immediately after Jesus was baptized in water by John the Baptist, Jesus was led into the wilderness by the Spirit to be tempted by the devil. Jesus had been fasting for forty days and was tired and hungry. So as our perfect Example, what did Jesus do when faced with temptation? He did the same exact thing that we should do—He turned to the Scripture:

> Then Jesus was led up by the Spirit into the wilderness to be tempted by the devil. And after fasting forty days and forty nights, he was hungry. And the tempter came and said to him, "If You are the Son of God, command these stones to become loaves of bread." But He answered, "It is written, 'Man shall not live by bread alone, but by every word that comes from the mouth of God.'" Then the devil took Him into the holy city and set him on the pinnacle of the temple and said to him, "If You are the Son of God, throw yourself down, for it is written, 'He will command His angels concerning You,' and 'On their hands they will bear you up, lest you strike your foot against a stone.'" Jesus said to him, "Again it is written, 'You shall not put the Lord your God to the test.'" Again, the devil took him to a very high mountain and showed him all the kingdoms of the world and their glory. And he said to him, "All these things I will give you, if you will fall down and worship me." Then Jesus said to him, "Be gone, Satan! For it is written, 'You shall worship the Lord

your God and him only shall you serve.'" Then the devil left him, and behold, angels came and were ministering to him (Matt. 4:1-11).

Jesus was tempted by the devil through the three weaknesses of humanity: "the desires of the flesh and the desires of the eyes and pride of life" (1 John 2:16). In response, Jesus quoted three times from the book of Deuteronomy. Jesus is the Word, and Jesus is the Truth; but when tested, He showed us the power of the Word of God. I want to be clear about something: many people use this passage to try and support a false teaching that quoting the Scriptures has a mystical power that if you say them out loud, its power is set free in the universe to work on your behalf. This is not what we should learn from this passage. This is all about understanding and applying God's Word. It's about counteracting lies with truth. It is about hearing, perceiving, and doing!

> But be doers of the word, and not hearers only, deceiving yourselves. For if anyone is a hearer of the word and not a doer, he is like a man who looks intently at his natural face in a mirror. For he looks at himself and goes away and at once forgets what he was like. But the one who looks into the perfect law, the law of liberty, and perseveres, being no hearer who forgets but a doer who acts, he will be blessed in his doing (Jas. 1:22-25).

When we quote Scripture to overcome temptation, we are meditating on something we learn, perceive, and believe. The power to overcome sin through the Scripture isn't that it changes our circumstance or our situation but that Scripture transforms us and changes us. Scripture "[makes] wise the simple," makes us clean, and converts the heart into salvation.

THE RICH MAN AND LAZARUS

> "There was a rich man who was clothed in purple and fine linen and who feasted sumptuously every day. And at his gate was laid

a poor man named Lazarus, covered with sores, who desired to
be fed with what fell from the rich man›s table. Moreover, even
the dogs came and licked his sores. The poor man died and was
carried by the angels to Abraham›s side. The rich man also died
and was buried, and in Hades, being in torment, he lifted up his
eyes and saw Abraham far off and Lazarus at his side. And he
called out, 'Father Abraham, have mercy on me, and send Lazarus
to dip the end of his finger in water and cool my tongue, for I am
in anguish in this flame.' But Abraham said, 'Child, remember that
you in your lifetime received your good things, and Lazarus in like
manner bad things; but now he is comforted here, and you are in
anguish. And besides all this, between us and you a great chasm
has been fixed, in order that those who would pass from here to
you may not be able, and none may cross from there to us.' And he
said, 'Then I beg you, father, to send him to my father›s house—
for I have five brothers—so that he may warn them, lest they also
come into this place of torment.' But Abraham said, 'They have
Moses and the Prophets; let them hear them.' And he said, 'No,
father Abraham, but if someone goes to them from the dead, they
will repent.' He said to him, 'If they do not hear Moses and the
Prophets, neither will they be convinced if someone should rise
from the dead'" (Luke 16:19-31).

In this parable, Jesus talks about a rich man who is left unnamed and
a poor beggar, named Lazarus, who is. In the story, the rich man lives an
extravagant life where he wants for nothing. But Lazarus, on the other hand,
suffered and starved and begged for crumbs from the rich man's table. The
indictment against the rich man was obviously that he had more than enough
to feed this poor beggar, whom he must have known because it says that he
sat outside the gate of his house every day.

Feeding the poor and doing good deeds isn't what saves us, but it is
evidence that your heart has been transformed by salvation. Jesus said that
the entire Law and Prophets could be summed up with two commands: "'love
the Lord your God with all your heart and with all your soul and with all your

mind and with all your strength . . . [and] love your neighbor as yourself'" (Mark 12:30-31). Also, in the gospel of Matthew, Jesus talks about separating His sheep from the goats, who will be cast into the lake of fire.

> And the King will answer them, "Truly, I say to you, as you did it to one of the least of these my brothers, you did it to me." Then he will say to those on his left, "Depart from me, you cursed, into the eternal fire prepared for the devil and his angels. For I was hungry and you gave me no food, I was thirsty and you gave me no drink, I was a stranger and you did not welcome me, naked and you did not clothe me, sick and in prison and you did not visit me." Then they also will answer, saying, "Lord, when did we see you hungry or thirsty or a stranger or naked or sick or in prison, and did not minister to you?" Then he will answer them, saying, "Truly, I say to you, as you did not do it to one of the least of these, you did not do it to me." And these will go away into eternal punishment, but the righteous into eternal life (Matt. 25:40-46).

The rich man had lived for himself in wealth and privilege, and he wasn't compassionate to his neighbor when it was in his power to do so. It wouldn't change his life one bit to help Lazarus, but his heart was hard and selfish, which is evidence that he had not responded to the Gospel in repentance for his sin. His lack of love and compassion toward Lazarus showed that the love of God wasn't in him. When they both died, Lazarus went to paradise where he found comfort and peace, but the rich man went to Hell, where he was tormented continuously.

Now the tables have turned, and it is the rich man who begs. He cries out and asks Father Abraham to have Lazarus just put some water on his tongue to soothe his pain and give him just a second of relief, but this is impossible because there is an unbridgeable chasm between Heaven and Hell. In the end, he realizes that there was no hope for him, and still selfish and entitled, he asks Father Abraham to send Lazarus on an errand back to the world of the living. He asks that Lazarus might go and warn his brothers of what awaits them if they don't repent and change their ways, but Abraham says, "They have Moses and the prophets; let them listen to them." The phrase "Moses and the prophets," or the "the law and the prophets" would have been a very familiar phrase to the Jews listening to this parable. This is just another way of saying the Scripture. "Moses and the prophets" refers to the Old Testament; they didn't have the New Testament yet because they were still living it out.

Jesus was using this parable to tell his followers that the Scriptures are sufficient. We don't reject God because of a lack of evidence or lack of miracles; we reject God because our hearts are hard, and we love sin. Everything we need for salvation, life, and godliness is revealed in Scripture.

The rich man didn't see the value of God's Word; he didn't see it in his lifetime and still didn't in his judgment. Those who reject God will never see the value of His Word, even when they are being judged according to it in eternal condemnation. The rich man, not seeing the sufficiency and authority of Scripture, instead asks for a miracle. But if they didn't listen to Moses and the prophets, why would they listen to Lazarus?

The idea of this is foreign to most people because they reject even what the Scripture says about the heart of a sinful man that suppresses the knowledge of God for the sake of their own wickedness. This is the Law of God. It's in the perfect Law of the Lord that we see our need for a Savior, and through the prophets, we are called to repent and weep and mourn over our sin. But there is One Who has risen from the dead, "the Lamb of God, who takes away the sin of the world" (John 1:29). We not only have the Law and Prophets, but we also have the One Who has risen from the dead revealed in the Gospels, explained in the epistles, and promised to return in His revelation. We are without excuse.

The Word of God is a gift that brings either condemnation or freedom, that pronounces death or leads us to life. The Scripture is perfect because God is perfect. It reveals to us the Law by which we are judged and the Gospel by which we are saved, but most importantly, the Bible reveals to us the image of the invisible God, our Savior Jesus Christ. The Scripture is timeless, lacking nothing, uniquely equipped to help us correct, rebuke, and encourage. On it, we weigh all things; by it, we judge all things; and by it and according to it, all will be judged. God-breathed, inerrant, and pure, the sacred words of God as revealed in the Scripture are ultimately and supremely authoritative and fully sufficient.

"The grass withers, the flower fades when the breath of the Lord blows on it;
surely the people are grass. The grass withers, the flower fades,
but the word of our God will stand forever."

Isa. 40:7-8

CHAPTER 10

TO LIVE IS CHRIST: TO DIE IS GAIN

What then? Only that in every way, whether in pretense or in truth, Christ is proclaimed, and in that I rejoice. Yes, and I will rejoice, for I know that through your prayers and the help of the Spirit of Jesus Christ this will turn out for my deliverance, as it is my eager expectation and hope that I will not be at all ashamed, but that with full courage now as always Christ will be honored in my body, whether by life or by death. For to me to live is Christ, and to die is gain.

Phil. 1:18-21

John Piper said, "The only people that are of any worldly good in this life are those that are so radically heavenly minded that they are free of this world and free from stuff . . . stuff is killing us."[2] Paul takes it further when he says, "For me to live is Christ, and to die is gain." First, we must realize that magnifying and glorifying Christ was the great joy of Paul's life. And one of the main ways this joy was manifest was in the lives of other believers who he helped to build up and encourage. To live in Christ and for Christ, doing His work, is the joy that drove him. But on the other hand, Paul also knew that the reward that awaited him in death far outweighed any joy or reward that he would experience in this life.

---

2   John Piper, "How the Supremacy of Christ Creates Radical Christian Sacrifice," April 25, 2018, T4G 2008, YouTube, 1:04:54, https://www.youtube.com/watch?v=rdWsnr7qit4.

If I am to live in the flesh, that means fruitful labor for me. Yet which I shall choose I cannot tell. I am hard pressed between the two. My desire is to depart and be with Christ, for that is far better. But to remain in the flesh is more necessary on your account. Convinced of this, I know that I will remain and continue with you all, for your progress and joy in the faith, so that in me you may have ample cause to glory in Christ Jesus, because of my coming to you again (Phil. 1:22-26).

Paul truly understood that his death would do nothing but hasten his reward which freed him to be very effective and fruitful in this life. A Christian who doesn't understand this will not be fruitful. The fear of failure, the fear of man, and the fear of death will limit what you will be able to accomplish. Just like the love of money, the love of your life, selfish ambition, and a lack of faith will. Paul wanted to be with Christ but not until his usefulness for Him here on Earth had run its course.

If you truly believe Paul's statement in Philippians, your life will look conspicuously different than the world around you. The reason we live is to forward the Gospel of Christ and to glorify God because for us, death means to have our eternal reward. Those who truly have Christ will consider it pure joy when they face trials of many kinds because they know it is perfecting their faith and producing perseverance in them. If you are seeking your reward and treasure in this life, it is an indicator that maybe your treasure is in the here and now and not in the life to come and definitely not in Christ.

***

"For whoever would save his life will lose it,
but whoever loses his life for my sake will save it."

Luke 9:24

Luke 9:24 doesn't say to ask Jesus into your heart or let Him be a part of your life. It says that we are to lose our lives. To have the honor to lose your life in Christ is the greatest privilege of the Christian life! Being a Christian is like joining an elite army from which you will never be discharged. It is like becoming a lifelong bond servant to the Master and King of the universe. The life of a Christian is radically and fully devoted to the service of Christ. The true Christian should be able to say that about himself, and the person observing your life from the outside should be able to say that as well. To truly know Christ is life-transforming and all-consuming. The causal nature of most people's associations with Christ looks nothing like losing their life. True Christianity isn't causal; it can't be. Nothing that involves eternity, Heaven and Hell, a bloody death on a cross, and resurrection from the dead could be. It's either everything, or it's nothing. But it's definitely not causal.

***

"I want you to know, brothers, that what has happened to me has really served to advance the gospel, so that it has become known throughout the whole imperial guard and to all the rest that my imprisonment is for Christ."

Phil. 1:12-13

Paul wrote the letter to the Philippians while sitting in a jail cell. He was there because of preaching the Gospel and his missionary endeavors. It immediately becomes clear just a few lines into his letter that his main concern was for the churches that he helped plant and the people who made up those churches. But his main focus was the proclamation of the Gospel and representing Jesus well in whatever state in which he found himself. Paul was content because his strength and joy were in Christ, and he knew that death would be his greatest reward.

Serving to advance the Gospel was the point and mission of Paul's entire life. Can you say the same? Will you happily suffer for the cause of Christ? This is a very important question because it says a lot about the true state of your soul. Richard Wurmbrand, the founder of the ministry Voice of the Martyrs, spent fourteen years in a Romanian prison because he stood up for Christ against the communist regime there. He was tortured and mistreated severely and could have been freed several times over the years if he simply would have been willing to deny Christ and endorse the Communist party. He never did. A reporter asked him years later how it was that this experience didn't break his faith in God. And this was his response: "A faith that can be destroyed by suffering is not faith."[3]

Today in American church culture, most professing Christians have a hard time talking about the realities of Hell or the exclusive nature of the Gospel when sharing their faith. That's in the rare cases they actually do share their faith. We are much too concerned with being perceived as judgmental or being misunderstood to boldly speak the truth. We are far too worried about our own comfort and personal rights to live for Christ in a way that might draw attention to us in a negative light. We believe that unless the world receives us well, we won't be able to win it over; but sadly, the opposite is true. Your supposed convictions have been weighed by your life and actions and found wanting, and maybe it is you who still needs to be won over.

LIVING A LIFE WORTHY OF THE GOSPEL

Paul said in Philippians 1 that his only desire was that either through his life or by his death that his body might honor Christ. This is not an extreme response to Christ; this is a right response and the only true response to the grace we have been given in the Gospel. If death means we will be with Him in complete peace, have fullness of joy, and be completely free from the bondage of sin forever and ever, then it should be our life's greatest joy to pour out every drop of this life He has given us for His glory.

Have you ever heard the phrase, "Don't be so heavenly minded that you're no earthly good"? The truth is, as a Christian, the opposite is actually true. People who are focused on self, stuff, and the things of this world aren't very useful for drawing people to God. Being a slightly more moral version of the pagan chasing the treasures of this world doesn't make a Christian stand out

---

3   Richard Wurmbrand, *If Prison Walls Could Speak* (Living Sacrifice Book Co.: 1993).

like salt or light in this dark world. The only people who are of any earthly good in this life are those unpossessed by possessions, who have already died to this world and are living for the next.

At some point, if we really want to win people to the cause of Christ, we are going to have to unhinge from the love and treasure of this world and live lives of missionary sacrifice. Chasing prosperity and comfort and more and more stuff isn't going to draw anyone to Christ. It just shows the lost that we are really not much different than them and that we are basically living for the same things they are in this world.

First John 2:15 says, "Do not love the world or the things in the world." And Matthew 6:19 says, "Do not lay up for yourselves treasures on earth." So, do you love the world and the things in this world? And where is your treasure? Here in this life or in Christ and in the life to come? Jesus says it can't be both: "'For where your treasure is, there your heart will be also'" (Matt. 6:21).

What has your heart? It's very easy for us to lie to ourselves, but honestly examine your life and ask yourself these questions: what do I treasure? On what do I spend the majority of my thought life? On what do I spend the majority of my time? On what do I spend my money? What is my life actually about? What do people who know me think my life is about? The answers to these questions are great clues to what actually holds your heart.

***

"Count it all joy, my brothers, when you meet trials of various kinds,
for you know that the testing of your faith produces steadfastness.
And let steadfastness have its full effect, that you may be perfect and
complete, lacking in nothing."

Jas. 1:2-4

How do you know if your life is bearing fruit that says "to live is Christ"? Ask yourself this: do your chains, troubles, trials, and struggles somehow advance the Gospel of Jesus Christ?

While he was in jail, Paul was most concerned with making sure his imprisonment and the fact that he was in chains somehow forwarded the Gospel of Christ and brought glory to God. He was happy that the entire palace guard and everyone else knew that he was in chains for Christ. Paul spent much of his time in jail writing letters of encouragement to the churches he had helped plant. He wasn't focused on comfort or himself but on living his life in a way that was worthy of Christ and His Gospel.

**

"Only let your manner of life be worthy of the gospel of Christ, so that whether I come and see you or am absent, I may hear of you that you are standing firm in one spirit, with one mind striving side by side for the faith of the gospel."

Phil. 1:27

Whatever happens, we must be salt and light and live our lives in a way worthy of the Gospel. Christ was beaten, mocked, tortured, and eventually killed for you. Live your life accordingly. We are now the trusted messengers of the very message that saved us from destruction—the most precious message in history. A message that brings eternal life to those who are damned. The true disciple doesn't ask questions like, "Why me, God? Haven't I served you?" or say things like, "I don't deserve this." The true disciple who trusts the Lord with his life and eternity asks the question, "How can my suffering, my trouble, and my pain forward the Gospel?" This is why Paul said, "To live is Christ, and to die is gain"—because the life a disciple of Jesus has truly given their life to Him to use as He sees fit for His kingdom purposes and to forward the Gospel.

JOY IN SUFFERING

True joy is supernatural; it is an outworking and evidence of the Spirit of God living in you. Nothing in this world can give you joy, and nothing in this world can take it away. The joy and peace of the Lord is present in your life during the good times and the bad. In fact, it is often more apparent when times are hard because having joy and peace during trial isn't a logical and normal reaction. We find joy in suffering, persecution, and trial for a few reasons. For one, it produces perseverance, like it tells us in James 1. Also, it works out the image of Christ in us. And our unwavering devotion to Christ in the midst of suffering brings much glory to God. As Paul said to the Philippians, "As it is my eager expectation and hope that I will not be at all ashamed, but that with full courage now as always Christ will be honored in my body, whether by life or by death" (Phil. 1:20).

This is what a surrendered life to the service of Christ looks like. Many people claim to have saving faith and relationship with Christ and say that they love Him. Don't be deceived! If your love for God is a love that is unwilling to suffer and sacrifice, it is no love at all. Now, don't confuse what I'm saying; I am not saying your love or lack of love for God somehow brings about salvation. Salvation is a free, unearned gift from God. What I *am* questioning is how someone who has been saved by God and overcome with His amazing grace could not love God. The answer is that he can't. Love is a fruit of the Spirit, and reciprocating the love God has shown us in the Gospel is an obvious byproduct of someone who has been reborn and transformed by the saving love and grace of God.

Christ is worthy, and our greatest joy and privilege should be suffering for the One Who sacrificed Himself to give us life because we love Him above all but also because we are fully convinced of what awaits us upon our death, our eternal reward. In the New Testament, the apostles were beaten and imprisoned for preaching the name of Jesus. On one such occasion in the book of Acts, Peter and John were imprisoned for preaching the Gospel, and during the night, an angel of the Lord released them and told them to go stand in the temple courts and preach the Gospel. Afterward, they were seized again and were almost put to death, but one of the teachers of the Law argued against it because he didn't want them to become martyrs and heroes and maybe start an uprising. So, the other teachers of the Law agreed and instead had them severely flogged and then released. What was their response to this? ""Then they left the presence of the council, rejoicing that they were counted worthy to suffer dishonor for the name. And every day, in the temple and from house to house, they did not cease teaching and preaching that the Christ is Jesus" (Acts 5:41-42).

A joyous embrace of Christian suffering is what shines like a bright light in a dark world. If Christianity is truly everything, then they had better see us living for it like we are ready and willing to die for it. The Christian life is about perseverance and endurance until the end. It is the Spirit of God that will sustain us if we are really His. Our endurance is about our love for God, but it is also that we truly believe the promises He has made in His Word to those who endure until the end. We will receive a crown of life; we will be in the fullness of His love, joy, and peace; we will reign with Him. Yes, we will reign with Christ if we will lay this life down in exchange for the next.

***

"If we endure, we will also reign with him; if we deny him, he also will deny us."

2 Timothy 2:12

Most who claim Christ wouldn't openly deny Him with their words, although some would if given the right circumstances. But your words and supposed convictions are proven true or false by your actions. If we say we love Christ but reject any part of His Word because of persecution or suffering or because we don't like it or culture doesn't like it, we are rejecting Christ because He is the Word.

In the Old Testament, Moses chose temporary affiliation for the glory of God over the treasures of this world when he left a life of privilege in the palace of Pharaoh to lead God's people out of Egypt through forty years in the wilderness and eventually to the Promised Land.

> By faith Moses, when he was grown up, refused to be called the son of Pharaoh's daughter, choosing rather to be mistreated with the people of God than to enjoy the fleeting pleasures of sin. He considered the reproach of Christ greater wealth than the treasures of Egypt, for he was looking to the reward (Heb. 11:24-26).

Moses, Peter, John, and Paul understood life through the lens of eternity. These were men who saw the Lord, knew the Lord, and lived their lives accordingly. They lived lives that the words of Scripture considered worthy of the Gospel of Christ. Now, don't get me wrong; these men sinned and messed up along the way, but the core of their lives was laid down for the glory of God. Don't say you love God but are unwilling to deny yourself. Jesus never said following Him would be easy or feel good. But He did say in light of eternity, it would be worth it. The true Christian will gladly, even joyously, suffer for Christ, and it will be their greatest desire to obey Him.

***

"Whoever has my commandments and keeps them, he it is who loves me.
And he who loves me will be loved by my Father,
and I will love him and manifest myself to him."

John 14:21

Christian suffering and obedience to God don't earn us anything; it is merely evidence that your life in Christ and your love of Christ are genuine. But if your desire isn't to live a fully surrendered life that is pleasing to God, you might want to ask yourself these questions: do you really love God? And are you really His? Don't be deceived; biblical love is sacrificial and self-denying. And this kind of love is a fruit of the Spirit of Christ living in you. Christ Himself showed us what this looks like in His love toward us.

- "Greater love has no one than this, that someone lay down his life for his friends" (John 15:13).

- "But God shows his love for us in that while we were still sinners, Christ died for us" (Rom. 5:8).

- "'For God so loved the world, that he gave his only Son, that whoever believes in him should not perish but have eternal life. For God did not send his Son into the world to condemn the world, but in order that the world might be saved through him" (John 3:16-17).

***

"And if children, then heirs—heirs of God and fellow heirs with Christ,
provided we suffer with him in order that we may also be glorified with him."

Rom. 8:17

People who try to divorce the concept of Christian suffering from Christianity have to avoid much of the Bible and work hard to take it out of context to come up with that logic. If we are co-heirs with Christ, the Bible says we will suffer but that in the end, we will glory. If He didn't spare His own Son, why would we think we are above this? Remember, trial and suffering give us perseverance, conform us to Christ's image, and bring glory to our King. We are God's children and are part of the family of Christ. In the life to come, we will share in His glory but only if we are willing to share in His suffering in this life.

There is no exemption for suffering in this life; it rains on the just and unjust. But will you give your life away to let God use it for His glory and to forward His kingdom and His Gospel? In blessing and in suffering, through good times and bad times, will you keep your eyes fixed on "Jesus, the founder and perfecter of our faith" (Heb. 12:2)? He is our Reward and our Treasure, and nothing in this life is more valuable than He. He is worth any sacrifice or cost. Paul says in Philippians 1 that the opportunity to suffer for the cause of Christ is a gift just like believing in God is.

***

"For it has been granted to you that for the sake of Christ you should not only believe in him but also suffer for his sake."

Phil. 1:29

Knowing Christ has been granted to us like a gift. To people on the outside, this doesn't sound like a gift because the value of the Lord is veiled to them. The joy of proclaiming the Gospel is the opportunity to unveil Christ and see men and women wake up to His majesty and glory. Of course, it is the Spirit God that draws men and women to salvation, not our words. But as obedient servants proclaiming His Word, we are given the great honor of being His messengers and the instruments used through God's sovereignty to draw them in.

Although there are trials and suffering in the Christian life, they will be swallowed up like a tear in the ocean when the glory of God is revealed in us. Paul says it is not even worth comparing this life with the next. People who are convinced of this live lives of great value for Christ and His kingdom. In Romans 8:18, Paul encourages, "For I consider that the sufferings of this present time are not worth comparing with the glory that is to be revealed to us."

"To live is Christ!" Once you truly know Christ, everything about life becomes about magnifying Him, bringing glory to Him, and drawing people to Him. The true Christian's life will look like this. Once you know, you know, and you will never be the same. "To die is gain." If the life of a true disciple is made joyful and complete by living in honor of the Savior, you love with all of your heart. Then, of course, death will be your greatest gain because in death, you will finally be with Him face to face in the absolute fullness of His love. And there is nothing that can ever separate those who are His from that love. In life and in death, we are more than conquerors through the One who saved us. He chose us, sought us, bought us, and saved us; and there is nothing in the highest Heaven or the deepest Hell that could ever snatch us from His hands. "To live is Christ, and to die is gain."

As it is written, "For your sake we are being killed all the day long; we are regarded as sheep to be slaughtered." No, in all these things we are more than conquerors through him who loved us. For I am sure that neither death nor life, nor angels nor rulers, nor things present nor things to come, nor powers, nor height nor depth, nor anything else in all creation, will be able to separate us from the love of God in Christ Jesus our Lord (Rom. 8:36-39).

CHAPTER 11

THE DAY OF THE LORD

"But the day of the Lord will come like a thief, and then the heavens will pass
away with a roar, and the heavenly bodies will be burned up and dissolved,
and the earth and the works that are done on it will be exposed."

2 Peter 3:10

It is impossible to write a book on Christian discipleship without discussing the day of the Lord. Any Christian apologetic or meaningful evangelism message that is void of the final judgment is lacking, at best. The Gospel itself is a message of salvation, but salvation from what? If we are being "saved," there must be something from which we are being saved. The reason many don't discuss this very important element of Christianity is because it undermines their flawed theology that focuses on love and grace at the expense of repentance from sin. In the Gospel, we are being saved from the wrath of God Himself—the wrath and judgment that He will pour out on all things found outside of Christ on the day of the Lord.

All things outside of Christ are subject to judgment and condemnation. Everything in existence was created by Him, for Him, and is subject to Him. This includes everything in creation. There is nothing that will not ultimately surrender to His sovereignty and authority. The day of the Lord isn't just about the wrath of God; it is also about the greatness and glory of our God. When Peter preached His first sermon on the day of Pentecost, His Gospel presentation centered around the day of the Lord, where he quotes from the book of Joel:

> "'And in the last days it shall be, God declares, that I will pour out my Spirit on all flesh, and your sons and your daughters shall prophesy, and your young men shall see visions, and your old men shall dream dreams; even on my male servants and female servants in those days I will pour out my Spirit, and they shall prophesy. And I will show wonders in the heavens above and signs on the earth below, blood, and fire, and vapor of smoke; the sun shall be turned to darkness and the moon to blood, before the day of the Lord comes, the great and magnificent day. And it shall come to pass that everyone who calls upon the name of the Lord shall be saved'" (Acts 2:17-21).

The day of the Lord will be great and glorious. The King of all kings will be glorified in all of Heaven and in all the Earth. God's people will be delivered and saved for His glory, and all of creation will worship Him. But God will also be glorified in the destruction of His enemies. This is something that most Christians in our culture don't believe or at least don't want to talk about, but it is as true as everything else written in the Scripture. God is full of love and mercy, but to those who reject the sacrifice of Christ and the salvation it provides, those people's destruction will bring glory to the God they rejected. The Bible says it's not His wish that any should perish but that all would have eternal life; but to those who are not saved from the due penalty of their sin, they will receive eternal judgement and condemnation. In the book of Revelation, it says that they rejoice in Heaven as the smoke of their enemies goes up forever and ever.

> After this I heard what seemed to be the loud voice of a great multitude in heaven, crying out, "Hallelujah! Salvation and glory and power belong to our God, for his judgments are true and just; for he has judged the great prostitute who corrupted the earth

with her immorality, and has avenged on her the blood of his servants." Once more they cried out, "Hallelujah! The smoke from her goes up forever and ever" (Rev. 19:1-3).

SALVATION IN CHRIST

"There is therefore now no condemnation for those who are in Christ Jesus.
For the law of the Spirit of life has set you free in Christ Jesus
from the law of sin and death."

Rom. 8:1-2

In Romans 8:1, the apostle Paul delivers one of the most profound statements in the entire Bible. So, it is true to say all things outside of Christ are subject to condemnation; it is equally valid to say the opposite is true. For those who are in Christ, there is no condemnation. So, what does it mean to be fully found in His salvation? There is a story in the Old Testament that paints a picture of what it means to be in Christ as a historical and prophetic foreshadowing of the day of the Lord.

In Genesis 6-9, we are given the account of Noah and the Great Flood. It says in Genesis 6 that wickedness abounded in the Earth and that God was going to bring judgment and wipe out the entire human race. But one man found favor with the Lord, and He chose to spare him. That man was Noah. It says, "Noah was . . . blameless. Noah walked with God" (Gen. 6:9).

The world was wicked, and the Scripture says that the people only thought of evil all the time. God warned Noah that he was going to flood the entire world. He commanded him to build a massive ark and, when it was complete, to fill it with a pair of every kind of animal and his family. They would all be spared from the coming judgment. All who were in the ark would be saved. It took about 120 years to build the ark.

"By faith Noah, being warned by God concerning events as yet unseen, in reverent fear constructed an ark for the saving of his household. By this he condemned the world and became an heir of the righteousness that comes by faith" (Heb. 11:7). All who were in the ark were saved from the wrath and judgment of God. Don't kid yourself about Who God is; He hates sin so much that He destroyed all of humanity, except for eight people. God is holy, and there is no way to overstate that. God's rebellious and wayward creation deserved destruction, but in His mercy, He gave a singular, loving way of escape. Yet the wicked rejected it. To be in Christ is like being in the ark; you are saved from God's condemnation and judgment. Peter uses the example of the flood when speaking of the coming day of the Lord's final judgment for the wicked and salvation for the righteous.

> For if God did not spare angels when they sinned, but cast them into hell and committed them to chains of gloomy darkness to be kept until the judgment; if he did not spare the ancient world, but preserved Noah, a herald of righteousness, with seven others, when he brought a flood upon the world of the ungodly; if by turning the cities of Sodom and Gomorrah to ashes he condemned them to extinction, making them an example of what is going to happen to the ungodly (2 Peter 2:4-6).

We live in a time where people live in open and unrepentant wickedness; secular atheism is seen as logical wisdom; and we use the religion of science to judge the value and truth of God's own Word. People scoff and mock at the creation account, or the idea of a worldwide flood, or a sovereign God Who is coming back to bring judgment on the unrepentant wicked and to claim His bride, the Church. Many people who claim to be Christians so easily tolerate this blasphemy and do nothing to stand up to it. Like Noah, we must live blameless lives and obediently preach righteousness and the Gospel as the world scoffs and mocks us.

Noah took God at His Word, believed Him, and obeyed Him. He spent 120 years building the ark and pointing to it as the only way to be saved from the coming judgment. We, too, must obey God and spend our lives pointing to the Gospel of Jesus Christ as the only way of salvation from the coming eternal judgment. To be in Christ means that we are saved by grace alone, through faith alone, in Christ alone, according to the Scripture alone, all for the glory of God alone.

***

Knowing this first of all, that scoffers will come in the last days with scoffing, following their own sinful desires. They will say, "Where is the promise of his coming? For ever since the fathers fell asleep, all things are continuing as they were from the beginning of creation." For they deliberately overlook this fact, that the heavens existed long ago, and the earth was formed out of water and through water by the word of God, and that by means of these the world that then existed was deluged with water and perished. But by the same word the heavens and earth that now exist are stored up for fire, being kept until the day of judgment and destruction of the ungodly.

2 Peter 3:3-7

I am sure Peter used the comparison of the flood when speaking of the coming judgment of the Lord because he had heard it before when Jesus was preaching during His earthly ministry. What makes Jesus' comparison so much more compelling, though, is the fact that He is the very God Who sent the flood during the time of Noah. This the kindness and mercy of God—to use His past judgment as a warning to us. We have evidence that God is serious and will keep His promises toward humanity. To those who humbly heed His warning, He promises salvation and grace; but to those who harden their hearts and ignore the warning, He promises judgment and condemnation. God will always keep His Word. He warns us in Matthew 24:36-39:

> "But concerning that day and hour no one knows, not even the angels of heaven, nor the Son, but the Father only. For as were the days of Noah, so will be the coming of the Son of Man. For as in those days before the flood they were eating and drinking,

marrying and giving in marriage, until the day when Noah entered the ark, and they were unaware until the flood came and swept them all away, so will be the coming of the Son of Man."

Leaving out Hell, eternal suffering, and the righteous judgment and wrath of God when presenting the Gospel because we want to be loving or kind is like going into a burning house and calmly telling people they should go outside because it's a beautiful day, rather than telling them to get out of the house because it is on fire. It is because of love we preach the truth and repentance from sin. It is because of love we urgently preach the Gospel and the full counsel of God according to the Scripture. The house is on fire, and it's burning down fast. Get out while there is still time!

Once, when I was invited to preach at a church, I shared a message on the Beatitudes from the Sermon on the Mount that Jesus preached in Matthew 5:1-12. When I was finished preaching, a man in attendance told me that it had been a long time since he had heard an old-fashioned "fire and brimstone" message. I was perplexed by this statement because I hadn't preached on Hell, final judgment, or anything close to that.

When I asked him why he thought it was that type of message, he said that when I talked about the Gospel, I said unrepentant sinners would not inherit the Kingdom of God but instead would be cast into the Lake of Fire. That one statement made my entire message different from what he was used to hearing.

The Gospel preached in many churches today is void of the Gospel and the truths attached to it. When you simply preach the Scriptures in context, it seems harsh to many people today because quite often, they have been presented with a very different message. Often, when we preach biblical truth in love, we are called judgmental. But don't mistake a warning as judgment. Judgment is what comes to those who don't heed the warning.

Jesus will come back "like a thief in the night" (1 Thess. 5:2), "in a moment, in the twinkling of an eye" (1 Cor. 15:52). Even if you don't live to see it, either way, you are going to stand before the judgment seat of Christ very soon.

No one is promised tomorrow. "For you are a mist that appears for a little time and then vanishes" (Jas. 4:14).

Now concerning the times and the seasons, brothers, you have no need to have anything written to you. For you yourselves are fully aware that the day of the Lord will come like a thief in the night. While people are saying, "There is peace and security," then sudden destruction will come upon them as labor pains come upon a pregnant woman, and they will not escape (1 Thess. 5:1-3).

As humans, we desire peace, safety, and comfort, often at the expense of reality and truth. Even if we don't openly deny the truth, we suppress and ignore the truth, hoping to postpone it. This is the disease of our culture, never-ending amusement that helps us postpone and escape reality. Many openly deny reality and any form of absolute truth. Our culture is drowning in quippy little sayings and social media memes that are not connected to any body of work or any coherent reality or logical train of thought. The idea that we will stand before God at any moment and give an account of our life is the furthest thing from our mind. Once we are reborn into Christ, our eyes are open to reality, and we live a different life than we did when we were blind to the truth. There is no person more aware of reality than the biblical Christian. Knowing the truth, how, then, can we just go on as if nothing has changed when everything has changed? The only real reasons you would ignore this is because either you don't really believe, or you don't care.

The message of warning Jesus gives throughout the New Testament is as clear as the sky on a summer day. To ignore it, you must willfully close your eyes, but even then, you can see the brightness as it invades your closed eyelids. We will be without excuse on the day of judgment because the Scriptures warn us that Jesus Himself gave very clear warnings; nature itself testifies to the existence and glory of God; and we have the imprint of the image of God on our own consciences.

A CROWN OF RIGHTEOUSNESS

"Henceforth there is laid up for me the crown of righteousness, which the Lord,
the righteous judge, will award to me on that day, and not only to me but also
to all who have loved his appearing."

2 Tim. 4:8

For the true follower of Jesus, the day of the Lord is what we are longing for and what we are living for. Here is a very important question: do you long for His appearing, or are you at home in this world? Jesus is the righteous judge, and He dispenses justice perfectly. His justice is so perfect and just that on the day of the Lord, even the damned will acknowledge the fairness of His judgments. For those of us who are truly in Christ, we long for His appearing and the day He rescues us from this fallen world and "the sin which clings so closely" (Heb. 12:1). We also long to see Him face to face, to bow down at His feet and worship "the Lamb of God, who takes away the sin of the world" (John 1:29). Knowing that we are being saved, we are overjoyed for His return.

To be crowned with the right standing before God is the gift of all eternity. I believe that we will know to an even deeper degree on that day how precious a gift the grace of God truly is. Having a deep understanding and appreciation of the next life shapes us for how we live in this life. Matthew 5:6 says, "'Blessed are those who hunger and thirst for righteousness, for they shall be satisfied." In this life, we are justified before God the moment we are reborn in Christ. Sanctification is progressive over the course of a lifetime, but justification is instant. How glorious will it be on that day when we are counted as righteous by God in His presence because of what Christ did for us on the cross! And we will be forever grateful to Christ, realizing that the crown of righteousness we received rightfully belongs to Jesus—as do we and as do all things. In fact, Revelation 4:10-11 says:

> The twenty-four elders fall down before him who is seated on the throne and worship him who lives forever and ever. They cast

their crowns before the throne, saying, "Worthy are you, our Lord and God, to receive glory and honor and power, for you created all things, and by your will they existed and were created."

What a privilege it is to proclaim the glory of God in this life—in opposition, in suffering, through trial—knowing that one day we will stand with Him as He unveils His glory to all creation, and to see the majesty of the new heaven and the new earth unfold before our eyes. I don't see how anyone who truly believes this could be saddened in the least to see this corrupt and sinful world pass away. Every loss in this life should always be compared to the all-surpassing worthiness of Jesus Christ.

SHEEP AND GOATS

Either we are for Him, or we are against Him; there is no middle ground. Jesus is coming back to claim His bride, the Church; and once that day comes, it will be too late. In the Olivet Discourse in Matthew 24-25, Jesus tells us that although no one knows the exact day or hour of His return, there would be signs: wars and rumors of war, natural disasters, famine, false prophets, and false messiahs. He also said that true disciples would endure trials, tribulation, and persecution.

Jesus Himself gives us three parables that tell us to be prepared for His return: the parable of the foolish servant and the wise servant, the parable of the ten virgins, and the parable of the talents—all of which are about the soon-returning Messiah. We live in an era where, for the first time in hundreds of years, you could say that Christianity is in a true worldwide decline. Christians are being persecuted all across the world, and we are just steps away from losing religious liberty in what was once considered the freest culture in history. The least culturally relevant and popular thing to be is a true, biblical disciple of Jesus. Not the culturally acceptable, moderate, tolerant, lukewarm Christian consumer, but a true disciple. Jesus is coming back for a Church unstained by the world, who will persevere until the end. When He comes back, He will separate the wheat from the tares and sheep from the goats, and they will be assigned to either eternal life or eternal suffering.

> "When the Son of Man comes in his glory, and all the angels with him, then he will sit on his glorious throne. Before him will be gathered all the nations, and he will separate people one from another as a shepherd separates the sheep from the goats. And he will place the sheep on his right, but the goats on the left" (Matt. 25:31-33).

On the day that Christ comes in His glory to sit on His throne and judge the entire world, there will be a great separation between those who loved Him and served Him and everyone one else. For some, this will be the greatest moment of their life, but for most, it will be the most dreaded and frightening moment of their lives. Jesus spoke about this often; I wonder why most preachers don't? How can any true pastor who fears the Lord and loves people not mention this and often? "'Repent, for the kingdom of heaven is at hand'" (Matt. 3:2).

***

"Then the King will say to those on his right, 'Come, you who are blessed by my Father, inherit the kingdom prepared for you from the foundation of the world."

Matt. 25:34

As a disciple of Jesus, these words in Matthew 25:34 are the motivation of our lives. Everything we sacrificed, everything we gave up during our lives to follow Jesus will be made worthwhile in this moment. It is not that we are giving up the treasures of this world for nothing; we are giving up the treasures of this life for a treasure that is far more valuable than anything else. We are exchanging something temporal and fleeting for something that is sure and will never pass away. This is the faith we have as Christians—to lay down our lives joyfully and gladly because we aren't looking to find a home in this world, but instead, are "looking . . . to the city whose designer and builder is God" (Heb. 11:10). There is no greater joy and freedom than losing your life for Christ to find your life in Christ.

***

"Then he will say to those on his left, Depart from me, you cursed,
into the eternal fire prepared for the devil and his angels.'"

Matt. 25:41

Even as a follower of Christ, my heart sinks as I think about this moment—the moment where so many will suffer loss as they are separated for eternal fire and condemnation. This will not only include people who hated God and denied Him, but also those who were indifferent toward Him. This will include many who thought they were good people and believed that they lived good lives. But I believe those who will be the most shocked will be those who considered themselves Christians—those who followed a Jesus of their own invention, who thought their feelings were the Holy Spirit and followed them were they led. People whose security wasn't fully found in the Gospel of Jesus Christ. The masses who attended church, listened to Christian music, did good deeds, and let American church culture (rather than the Bible) dictate what it truly meant to follow Jesus. Matthew 7:21-23 warns:

> "Not everyone who says to me, 'Lord, Lord,' will enter the kingdom of heaven, but the one who does the will of my Father who is in heaven. On that day many will say to me, 'Lord, Lord, did we not prophesy in your name, and cast out demons in your name, and do many mighty works in your name?' And then will I declare to them, 'I never knew you; depart from me, you workers of lawlessness.'"

We so easily say today in the church, "I gave my life to Christ." We say it, but we give up nothing. Nothing about our lives changes, for the most part. To follow Jesus is to give up your life, die to yourself, give up control, and begin to live according to the Scriptures by the power of the Spirit. This is what it means to follow Jesus. Believing you can keep control of your life and follow Jesus is a lie straight from Hell, intended to draw you there.

***

"For whoever would save his life will lose it,
but whoever loses his life for my sake will find it."

Matt. 16:25

We will not regret anything we gave up for the Lord to be part of His kingdom in eternity, and people who live like they will do not know Him or see His worth. Nothing in this life could ever compare—nothing! The goal of my life is to pour out my entire life for my King and die empty. Words cannot express the joy and fulfillment we will experience on that day when we hear the words, "Well done, good and faithful servant . . . Enter into the joy of your master" (Matt. 25:21). Let anticipation of this moment motivate each and every decision you make in this life. The day of the Lord will be the most glorious and dreadful day in the history of the universe. Just like two countries at war, one side rejoices at the end, while the other mourns. The only difference is that in our case, the war is already over, and we are just awaiting the arrival of the conquering King. He is a good, merciful, and patient King. And He has sent out good news to His enemies. He will pardon them if they will lay down their arms in repentance and become faithful servants of His kingdom while He is still on the way. But don't mistake His patience and kindness for weakness because those who are unsurrendered when He arrives will be dealt with ever so severely for their rebellion, and their punishment will fit the crime. He is worthy!

"Therefore, beloved, since you are waiting for these, be diligent to be found by
him without spot or blemish, and at peace. And count the patience of our Lord
as salvation, just as our beloved brother Paul also wrote to you according to
the wisdom given him."

2 Peter 3:14-15

CHAPTER 12

THE REWARD OF HIS SUFFERINGS

Then I heard what seemed to be the voice of a great multitude, like
the roar of many waters and like the sound of mighty peals of thunder,
crying out, "Hallelujah! For the Lord our God the Almighty reigns.
Let us rejoice and exult and give him the glory, for the marriage of
the Lamb has come, and his Bride has made herself ready;
it was granted her to clothe herself with fine linen, bright and pure"—
for the fine linen is the righteous deeds of the saints.

Rev. 19:6-8

As true disciples and followers of Jesus Christ, He is our greatest Reward
and Treasure; but for Christ, His great reward and treasure is the Church
itself. In Scripture, the Church is referred to as the bride of Christ, and He is
referred to as the Bridegroom. This analogy makes clear the intimate nature
of our relationship with the Savior. Christ loves His Church and was willing
to lay down His life for her sake. Christ is jealous for His bride and will deal
harshly with those who mistreat her. This is also why we are warned against
false teachers so much. Jesus loves His Church and will build His Church,
and the gates of Hell will not prevail against it. May God have mercy on a
man who mistreats another man's bride. We know that the love of Jesus is
passionate and powerful; we also know that He is a jealous God. So how will
He treat those who swindle, mistreat, cause to stumble, or draw into adultery
the bride He loves?

The Church is the reward of Christ's sufferings, and we must reverence the bride as such. As His bride, we must live holy, pure, and undefiled lives as we await the Bridegroom's arrival. Also, as those entrusted with caring for the bride as brothers and sisters in the same body, we must take care of each other as well. Don't confuse the visible church with the true Church. There are many false prophets, false teachers, and false converts who claim Christ but do not really belong to Him. Often, these wolves in sheep's clothing will use terminology about keeping unity in the body of Christ to keep you from warning others about them. They will say things like, "Don't bring discord" or "You are causing division in the body." But this is taking the Scripture out of context just like the devil did in His temptation of Christ. We must be divisive when people preach a different gospel or twist the Scriptures. Out of love and care for the bride, we must cry out, "Wolf!" Jesus tells us to watch out for them and also lets us know that we will know them by their fruit.

> "Beware of false prophets, who come to you in sheep's clothing but inwardly are ravenous wolves. You will recognize them by their fruits. Are grapes gathered from thornbushes, or figs from thistles? So, every healthy tree bears good fruit, but the diseased tree bears bad fruit. A healthy tree cannot bear bad fruit, nor can a diseased tree bear good fruit. Every tree that does not bear good fruit is cut down and thrown into the fire. Thus you will recognize them by their fruits" (Matt. 7:15-20).

Not only are there false teachers and false prophets who want to ravage the bride, but equally as bad are those who defend them. There are many things we can disagree about and still be brothers and sisters in Christ; but the Gospel isn't one of them, and neither is the inerrancy of God's Word. A person who doesn't think anyone should ever be called out for being a false teacher is not someone you should trust because the Bible tells us the exact opposite. We must be sober in our judgments and make them according to Scripture and prayer with godly counsel and the Gospel in mind, but nonetheless, we must warn the sheep when we think we see a wolf among them.

The purpose of the Christian life is to worship the Lord in a biblically prescribed manner that is pleasing to God, and the purpose of the Church is to do this corporately. We were built to live in communion with God and community with each other. As believers, we must be unified under the truth and under Christ, Who is Truth. Unity among true believers is powerful and beautiful, not because there is power in our numbers as much as there is power in the common cord to which we cling, which is Christ. This unity is something that transcends the loyalty that we have to even our own natural family because we are now part of a new family that is eternal to whom we are connected through the saving grace of our Lord Jesus. Jesus Himself models this concept when dealing with His own earthly family:

> While he was still speaking to the people, behold, his mother and his brothers stood outside, asking to speak to him. But he replied to the man who told him, "Who is my mother, and who are my brothers?" And stretching out his hand toward his disciples, he said, "Here are my mother and my brothers! For whoever does the will of my Father in heaven is my brother and sister and mother" (Matt. 12:46-50).

Great evidence that you truly belong to God is that you identify with His elect more than you do with your earthly family. The love of God will be apparent in the love you have for God's people. Let me be clear, I am speaking about true Christians, not all people in the world. We do show God's love for those outside the Church, but we show it in an evangelistic way. Our loyalty as Christ's Church is first to God and then to each other.

***

Whoever says he is in the light and hates his brother is still in darkness.
Whoever loves his brother abides in the light, and in him there is no cause for

stumbling. But whoever hates his brother is in the darkness and walks in the
darkness, and does not know where he is going,
because the darkness has blinded his eyes.

1 John 2:9-11

The apostle John talks about this in His first epistle. He makes it clear that if you don't love your brother or sister in Christ, it is because you are not in Christ. Love is the first evidence, or fruit of the Spirit, verifying that the Spirit of God lives inside of you. This love we have for the Church and for each other is a gift given to us in regeneration; this is a gift given from God Himself when He gives us a new nature.

Through John's gospel and his epistles, he uses the imagery of darkness and light to make a clear distinction between those who are truly part of the family of God and those who are not. There is no greater juxtaposition than that of darkness and light. There is no more of a clear way of saying either you are in Christ, or you are not. Love for the Church and fellow believers is obviously something that is nonnegotiable, but it is really deeper than that. John is essentially describing two opposite natures—one that loves God and desires to please Him and one that loves sin and lives to please himself.

If you claim to be in the light but hate a brother or a sister, you are still in darkness, meaning you are not truly saved, and you do not really belong to Christ. Hatred for your fellow believer is evidence to that. That doesn't mean that you won't ever have disagreements with fellow believers or that you will never get upset with fellow believers. It means that although these things will happen, because of your common faith in Christ, your love for God and for each other should transcend your disagreement.

So, if you have been raised to life in Christ, and your eyes have been opened, and you have died to the treasures of this world and yourself, then what is left to stumble over? Nothing! The love of God transforms us; it gives us a supernatural love for the Church and our fellow believer. It makes us mourn for the lost who are perishing, even when they marginalize us and even when they mock and persecute us because our eyes are opened to a reality we know is not theirs. We see all things in life in light of the grace we have received from God in the Gospel. The true Church of Christ is unified by our deep love and commitment to our Savior and the Gospel by which He saved us. The Gospel is the unbreakable bond of the Church. We are united with Christ in His sufferings and in His death so that we may also be united with Him in His resurrection. As Philippians 3:10-11 says, "That I may know him and the power of his resurrection, and may share his sufferings, becoming like him in his death, that by any means possible I may attain the resurrection from the dead."

A CHURCH HATED BY THE WORLD

Another thing that unites the Church to Christ and us to each other is the fact that for the most part, the world will hate us. We live in holiness and obedience to God among their wickedness and preach a Gospel that says that no one is good and that outside of Christ, all will be condemned. That message sounds pretty offensive to a world that believes that they are mostly good. One thing that makes the cross of Christ so offensive is that it says that all of our effort and all of our goodness before a holy God are like filthy rags.

***

For this is the message that you have heard from the beginning, that we should love one another. We should not be like Cain, who was of the evil one and murdered his brother. And why did he murder him? Because his own deeds were evil and his brother's righteous. Do not be surprised, brothers, that the world hates you. We know that we have passed out of death into life, because we love the brothers. Whoever does not love abides in death. Everyone who hates his brother is a murderer, and you know that no murderer has eternal life abiding in him.

1 John 3:11-15

We are bound to each other by God's love but also by the world's hatred for us. Cain killed his brother because "he belonged to the evil one," and this was made evident by his jealousy of Abel. Abel's goodness exposed Cain's wickedness, and he hated him for it and eventually killed him. John tells us that the world will hate us. If you are light in the darkness, don't be surprised when the darkness hates you. The light of the holiness of your life and the light of the words of Scripture you speak will be upsetting to those who are hiding in the darkness of sin. Those of us who are in Christ repented because our sin was exposed by the Light. Jesus Christ is the Light of the world, and when we draw close to Him, His light exposes the sin of our life. When this happens, there are only two options: let the conviction that comes from the awareness of your sin draw you to repentance that leads to salvation or run away back into the dark like a roach or a rat that quickly flees when you flip on a light switch in a room. John 3:19-21 says:

> And this is the judgment: the light has come into the world, and people loved the darkness rather than the light because their works were evil. For everyone who does wicked things hates the light and does not come to the light, lest his works should be exposed. But whoever does what is true comes to the light, so that it may be clearly seen that his works have been carried out in God" (John 3:19-21).

Christian persecution has always been normative throughout the history of the Church. Although, it may not seem that way to many Christians in our culture today because we are inundated with churches that teach the exact opposite and have created a demonic gospel of personal accommodation. Instead of saying come and die, this gospel says you can have it your way. Honestly, that is why very often when trials come, we are caught off-guard because many have been taught that if you follow Christ, you should always be happy, healthy, and wealthy in this life. Certain times throughout history have been worse than others as far as regimes go, but in personal evangelism, it has been the same from the start. We preach the truth; the world hates the truth, so they persecute us. But Peter encourages us:

> Beloved, do not be surprised at the fiery trial when it comes upon you to test you, as though something strange were happening to you. But rejoice insofar as you share Christ's sufferings, that you may also rejoice and be glad when his glory is revealed. If you are insulted for the name of Christ, you are blessed, because the Spirit of glory and of God rests upon you (1 Peter 4:12-14).

As the Church, we are united with Christ in His sufferings, His death, and His resurrection. We will be tested with fire in this life, but for those who endure the test, they will be purified like silver or gold refined in the fire and set apart for His glory. We will rejoice and be glad when His glory is revealed because we are part of that glory as sons and daughters of God and co-heirs with Christ. Ultimately, we are blessed because despite persecution and a season of worldly suffering, the Spirit of glory and of God rests on you like an unquenchable fire, like a radiant light in the darkness, like a sinner whose sins were once red as scarlet but have now been washed white as snow.

WE ARE ONE BODY

"For just as the body is one and has many members, and all the members of the body, though many, are one body, so it is with Christ. For in one Spirit we were all baptized into one body—Jews or Greeks, slaves or free—and all were made to drink of one Spirit."

1 Cor. 12:12-13

There are not many churches but only one enduring Church that is made up of people from every tribe and nation in the world. We must always think of ourselves as being part of Christ's Church. The local church is simply an embassy that represents the kingdom of which we are a part. The idea of being kingdom-minded means that we are more concerned with the body of Christ as a whole than we are with our local church or ourselves. When we do anything as people or as a church, we must pause and ask ourselves what kingdom we are building. Is it our kingdom, our ministry, our life, or God's kingdom?

***

The eye cannot say to the hand, "I have no need of you," nor again the head to the feet, "I have no need of you." On the contrary, the parts of the body that seem to be weaker are indispensable, and on those parts of the body that we think less honorable we bestow the greater honor, and our unpresentable parts are treated with greater modesty, which our more presentable parts do not require. But God has so composed the body, giving greater honor to the part that lacked it, that there may be no division in the body, but that the members may have the same care for one another. If one member suffers, all suffer together; if one member is honored, all rejoice together.

1 Cor. 12:21-26

So very often, we rate what is important and what is valuable based on worldly standards. We sometimes fail to realize how important all members of the body of Christ are. All in the body of Christ have been chosen by God and saved by the grace of God; therefore, it is extremely foolish to boast or think more of oneself than you should. Even those who seem to serve a less visible function are equally necessary and valuable according to God. This is why James, the half-brother of Jesus, is so harsh toward favoritism of any kind within the Church.

> My brothers, show no partiality as you hold the faith in our Lord Jesus Christ, the Lord of glory. For if a man wearing a gold ring and fine clothing comes into your assembly, and a poor man in shabby clothing also comes in, and if you pay attention to the one who wears the fine clothing and say, "You sit here in a good

place," while you say to the poor man, "You stand over there," or, "Sit down at my feet," have you not then made distinctions among yourselves and become judges with evil thoughts? (Jas. 2:1-4).

Worldly status, material wealth, and personal accomplishments have nothing to do with your value as children of God. James makes it clear in his epistle that if you judge people based on the color of their skin, the amount of money they have, or who they are in society, you have a wicked heart and an evil mind. It takes the entire body to function and accomplish the work of the Lord in this world. The person who joyfully collects trash in the parking lot of your church is equally as valuable and important as the man who delivers the sermon on the stage. The person who passes out the food to the poor is needed just as much as the person who donated the money to buy the food. The person who takes care of the babies is just as necessary as the worship leader. We are all gifted in many different ways, and all these gifts are intended to bring glory to God, forward the Gospel, and benefit the Church of Christ. How about businessmen and women who conduct themselves with integrity in the community, glorify God with the work of their hands, and use their resources to support the work of the Lord? We could go on and on. Some preach; some teach; some encourage; some pray; some administrate some help; some cook; and some build. Because of this, the body of Christ is diverse, multi-faceted, and beautiful.

The Scripture commands us to meet together for corporate worship. It also lays out guidelines for what is God-honoring worship and what is not. It gives us guidelines for what kind of men pastors and deacons should be and gives instruction on how to administer church discipline. While it is very important to understand what the Church is, it is equally important to understand who the Church is and Whose the Church is. The Church is under the authority of one Head, Jesus Christ—not church traditions or church leaders, but Christ alone. Who is the Church? More often than not in the New Testament, the term *the church* is directed at a group of people, not a building or organization. We are the eternal body of Christ, and this supersedes everything else.

MISSIONS, THE HIGHEST CALL

"And they sang a new song, saying, 'Worthy are you to take the scroll and to open its seals, for you were slain, and by your blood you ransomed people for God from every tribe and language and people and nation.'"

Rev. 5:9

One of the greatest tragedies in life is someone who claims to know the Lord but doesn't see Him worthy of paying any price to make Him known. Christian discipleship is all about dying to self for the glory of God. This should be a great joy for the true believer to pour out their life for the glory of what we have found—a Treasure that far exceeds anything else, Jesus Christ. Because of this, there really is no greater call than that of missions.

***

"And He said to them, 'Go into all the world and proclaim the gospel to the whole creation.'"

Mark 16:15

The Great Commission is a commandment of our Savior to all who follow Him. As Christians, preaching the Gospel is the job of every believer, not just the pastor and the elder. It is the responsibility of every Christian to participate in missions, either to go or to support and send others to go. I believe every new convert should pray and ask God if He is calling them to go into the mission field. Not that I believe all are called to go, but the life of a true disciple is at God's disposal. Since the proclamation of the Gospel is one of the most important things in the Christian life, I believe that we should all pray that prayer where we tell God we are willing to go and do whatever He wills and ask Him to lead and direct us. Here is the question: Lord, do You want me to go, or do You want me to support those who do? I honestly don't think that there is any other position on this.

In 1792, William Carey, who later would become known as "the father of the modern missionary movement," challenged his Baptist congregation by saying it was the responsibility of all believers to help forward the Gospel to unreached places and to the ends of the Earth. Some men from this group went on to form an organization called the Particular Baptist Society for Propagating the Gospel Among the Heathen, and they appointed Carey and his friend John Thomas to go to India as missionaries. The next year, Carey said goodbye to his church in Leicester, England, and everything he had ever known and set out for India. Before they left, they had a sendoff service for Carey; and after the service, he had a meeting with four leaders of the missions society that was sending him and his friend. During this meeting, these four men promised that they would support him in honor of their great Master, Jesus Christ, and that they would support him and his missionary effort until the day they died.

Andrew Fuller later described that day with an analogy. He said that the mission to India seemed like a few men who considered going into a deep, unexplored mine, and it was as if Carey said, "Well, I will go down if you will hold the rope." So, in Fuller's mind, it was as if he and the other men were saying, "As long as we live, we shall not let go of that rope."

So, our choices are either to go down the well or hold the rope as someone else goes down the well because we must go and preach His gospel and make His name known in all the Earth.

***

"How beautiful upon the mountains are the feet of him who brings good news, who publishes peace, who brings good news of happiness, who publishes salvation, who says to Zion, 'Your God reigns.'"

Isa. 52:7

The point of all missions is two-fold, to make known the glorious name of Jesus known in all the Earth and to offer salvation from sin by and through His Gospel. Because we live in a land of individualism, it is easy to see why the idea of casting your life away for something more valuable than yourself isn't well-received. In our culture today, we are taught to value ourselves above all else. This is very apparent in the way we spend our time and money; this is apparent in the music and entertainment that sells; this is apparent in the fact that we are so selfish, we think it makes sense to kill babies through abortion because they might add inconvenience to our lives.

This is not to say that out of their abundance, people aren't willing to help various social needs from time to time that they deem important. They do this for a variety of reasons, but it isn't the same thing as the true Christian or the true Christian missionary. As sinners, we do good deeds for scores of reasons—because our emotions are invoked or because we believe in the idea of karma and "what goes around comes around." People give because it gives them a sense of fulfillment to think they are making a difference. Sometimes, it's because the cause has touched us personally, like giving to cancer research because our mom had cancer or giving to addiction recovery because our son struggles with addiction. Some do good deeds because it makes them feel better about themselves, or in their mind, they believe it somehow rights wrongs they have committed. Some do good to soothe their conscience. But the disciple of Christ does his works unto God for just one reason—because He is worthy!

The true Christian is compelled by something completely different. We have found a treasure that far surpasses anything else, including our own lives. And all we want is to use every drop of our lives to glorify Jesus, our God Who called us and saved us. The idea of dying to one's self to follow Jesus isn't just a metaphor; it is the resolve of the crucified Man to die so we might live. We need Gospel proclamation and Christian discipleship everywhere, not just in foreign lands and unreached people groups. But the Great Commission tells us we must go into the world and proclaim the Good News. Today, however, we prepare our kids for college and middle-class safety more than we do for missionary sacrifice. If your young adult or teenage child approached you and said, "After much fasting and prayer, I believe God has called me to be a missionary in Iran, Pakistan, or Northern India," what would you say? If you are a Christian parent, there is no higher honor you can have than realizing that your child has truly died to themselves and wants to pour their life out for Jesus and to make Him known throughout the Earth.

When the worthiness of Jesus is at the forefront of the Church, world missions thrive; but when a church is pointed inward, focusing on itself rather than viewing itself as an integral part of the body of Christ, missions suffer. When you hear people argue about world missions and say things like, "Why are we sending money and resources overseas when our nation has problems of its own?" there is a problem. This sort of logic shows a couple of things. First, that the person who says this doesn't really know what world missions are. Humanitarianism is an important part of missions, but the point and focus of world missions is the proclamation of the Gospel, church planting, and Christian discipleship; everything else is secondary. Also, it shows just how blind we really are to the fact that we are so very blessed in this country. How can we rest easy knowing that there is someone in the world who has not heard the name of Jesus?

The main objective of world missions is church planting. The idea of just making a Gospel proclamation, feeding some people, and leaving doesn't look much like the New Testament example of the Great Commission at all. The Church is Christ's most precious possession, so when we use our lives to steward and help increase Christ's Church, He is well-pleased. But we must remember that it is Christ Who builds His Church, and we are merely the servants He is using to do it. When missions thrive and churches grow because we are boldly and faithfully preaching the Gospel, teaching God's Word, and biblically governing the Church, that is a good thing. But if we are trying to grow the Church at the expense of any of those things, it isn't pleasing to God; it can't be.

Missions is the tip of the spear, making the name of Jesus known to the heathen is of the highest importance. How can we just go on living while knowing that somewhere in the world, there are people that have never heard His Name? But there also people in your town who don't know Who He is and people at your job that don't know Who He is—or what they think they know isn't based on biblical truth. If you are a Christian and the primary thing people know about you isn't that you are a disciple and follower of Christ, you probably need to examine your life. After all, we are called to be salt and light.

Missions is just churches planting churches, and the Church is the most important thing to Christ in this world. We are the reward of His sufferings! Christ died for a people that He has called unto Himself, and that purpose cannot and will not be thwarted. The entirety of successful Christian living hinges on this statement made by our Savior: "'For whoever would save his life will lose it, but whoever loses his life for my sake will find it'" (Matt. 16:25). Jesus is calling us to come and die to ourselves and to die to the temporal trappings of this world. A man who is dead to this world and all the things in this world can be used greatly by God.

DEATH OUTSIDE THE CAMP

For the bodies of those animals whose blood is brought into the holy places by the high priest as a sacrifice for sin are burned outside the camp. So Jesus also suffered outside the gate in order to sanctify the people through his own blood. Therefore let us go to him outside the camp and bear the reproach he endured. For here we have no lasting city, but we seek the city that is to come.

Heb. 13:11-14

Social, safe American Christianity is of no value to anyone, and honestly that kind of Christianity will never be able to survive persecution. In ancient times, most cities had gates and walls, which kept the people safe. Jerusalem had a gate, and it separated the people in the city from the danger outside. Outside the city walls were robbers and lepers. This is where the trash was dumped and where unholy and unclean things were discarded. This is also where the sin offering was burned. In Hebrews 13, the author explains the fact that the priest made sacrifices that were temporary and powerless to wholly and fully save us from our sin in the temple, which was inside the safety of the city walls. But the discarded bodies, along with all unclean things, were burned outside the city gate.

Ironically, the perfect "Lamb of God, who takes away the sin of the world" was sacrificed outside the city gate. He did this to make us holy; we have been justified, and we are being sanctified and, one day, will be glorified. But to share in His glory, we must also share in His suffering and bear His disgrace. In 1 Peter 4:13, we read, "But rejoice insofar as you share Christ's sufferings, that you may also rejoice and be glad when his glory is revealed."

The author of Hebrews calls to us to come and die, to deny ourselves, pick up our cross, and follow Him (Luke 9:23). But why would this be appealing to us? First, we realize that this life is just a foreshadowing of a life to come. We go outside the gate because once reborn, we realize that this is not our city, and this is not our world. We are merely pilgrims who are passing through. We are not, nor can we ever be, at home inside the safety of the city or at comfort in this world because we are looking for an eternal city created by God. We joyfully take on His disgrace and reproach because our eyes have been opened to the fact that Jesus is our Treasure. He is the Reward of all ages; He is the King of all kings. Unbreakable and unchanging, He makes intercession for us. Those who think this view is extreme don't see the enduring value of Christ. He is the final Prophet, our eternal Priest, and the forever reigning King! He is our Priest forever, not because of tradition or His ancestry but on the basis of His indestructible life.

> For it is evident that our Lord was descended from Judah, and in connection with that tribe Moses said nothing about priests. This becomes even more evident when another priest arises in the likeness of Melchizedek, who has become a priest, not on the basis of a legal requirement concerning bodily descent, but by the power of an indestructible life (Heb. 7:14-16).

His divinity cannot be overtaken by death because He is a priest forever in the order of Melchizedek. He is our Treasure, and we are His Reward! The doxology of the Church and the motivation behind missions, the fire that burns in the heart of every true lover of Christ, is to understand the worthiness that is Christ Jesus our Lord. Christian discipleship is joyfully flinging your life away for the glory of the God Who saved you. It is understanding there is nothing in this life that could ever compare to His splendor. We are the reward of His sufferings, and the point of the Christian life is to live to glorify Him, to conform to His image, and to make His name known in all the Earth. The hope of my life is that I can somehow pour my entire life out in service of Him and die empty for His glory.

ABOUT THE AUTHOR

Joshua West is a pastor, evangelist, and author. He currently serves as the Pastor and Program Manager of Sonrise Adult & Teen Challenge in Cache, Oklahoma. The goal and focus of his ministry is biblical preaching and teaching with a high view of God and the Scripture. He partners in life and ministry with his wife and best friend, Kiara. Their goal is to preach the gospel to all people, make disciples and bring glory to the name Jesus.

For more information about
Joshua West
and
Come and Die
please connect at:

www.joshuawest.net
www.facebook.com/pastorjoshuawest

HARD
Sayings

Reconciling the Cost of Discipleship
and the American Dream

JOSHUA WEST

"A blockbuster of a message to the church and to preachers . . . "

-Don Wilkerson, President, Teen Challenge, Inc.

Can American Christianity really reconcile itself to the hard sayings of Jesus and the teaching of Scripture, or have we invented a version suitable for mass consumption that agrees with our Western ideas of fairness, our so-called rights, and the all-important American dream?

In order to make God approachable, have we left out the parts of the New Testament we don't like?

Is there a cost to being a disciple of Jesus?

How do we reconcile the teachings of the Jesus we find in Scripture with the American Jesus we have created?

In *Hard Sayings: Reconciling the Cost of Discipleship and the American Dream*, pastor and international speaker Joshua West considers these questions and more, and he compares the parables, teachings, and person of Jesus Christ found in Scripture against the pop culture Jesus we have invented in the West.

Looking at the entertainment-driven, celebrity culture of the American church, West challenges the reader to reconcile what the Bible calls the cost of discipleship with the American dream.

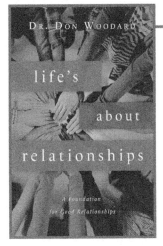

We interact with people every day whether it be with our coworkers, family, friends—life is filled with relationships! While not all relationships are good, with God's help, we can work to better our current and future relationships and overcome the effects of toxic relationships.

What does it mean to really live? Using Jesus' Sermon on the Mount as the blueprint, Dr. Martin Wiles answers some of the most pressing questions that Christians have about effective Christian living. In this powerful work, Dr. Wiles shares eighteen insights for learning how to pray, handle our anger, love our enemies, overcome worry, have a healthy marriage, and so much more. *Don't Just Live . . . Really Live* offers a practical approach for discerning how to live out the Bible in today's world.

Destination Hope is a must-read invaluable guide, offering hope and sound wisdom for your unpredictable, individual life journeys. Written by two of the wisest tried, tested, and true women of God—April White and Marilyn Nutter—you will see how each author poured out beautiful transparency. Like two best friends who've trailed the hard ground before you, April and Marilyn, seem to gently take you by the hand and lead you toward God's heart for healing.

Made in the USA
Coppell, TX
28 October 2021

64823801R00118